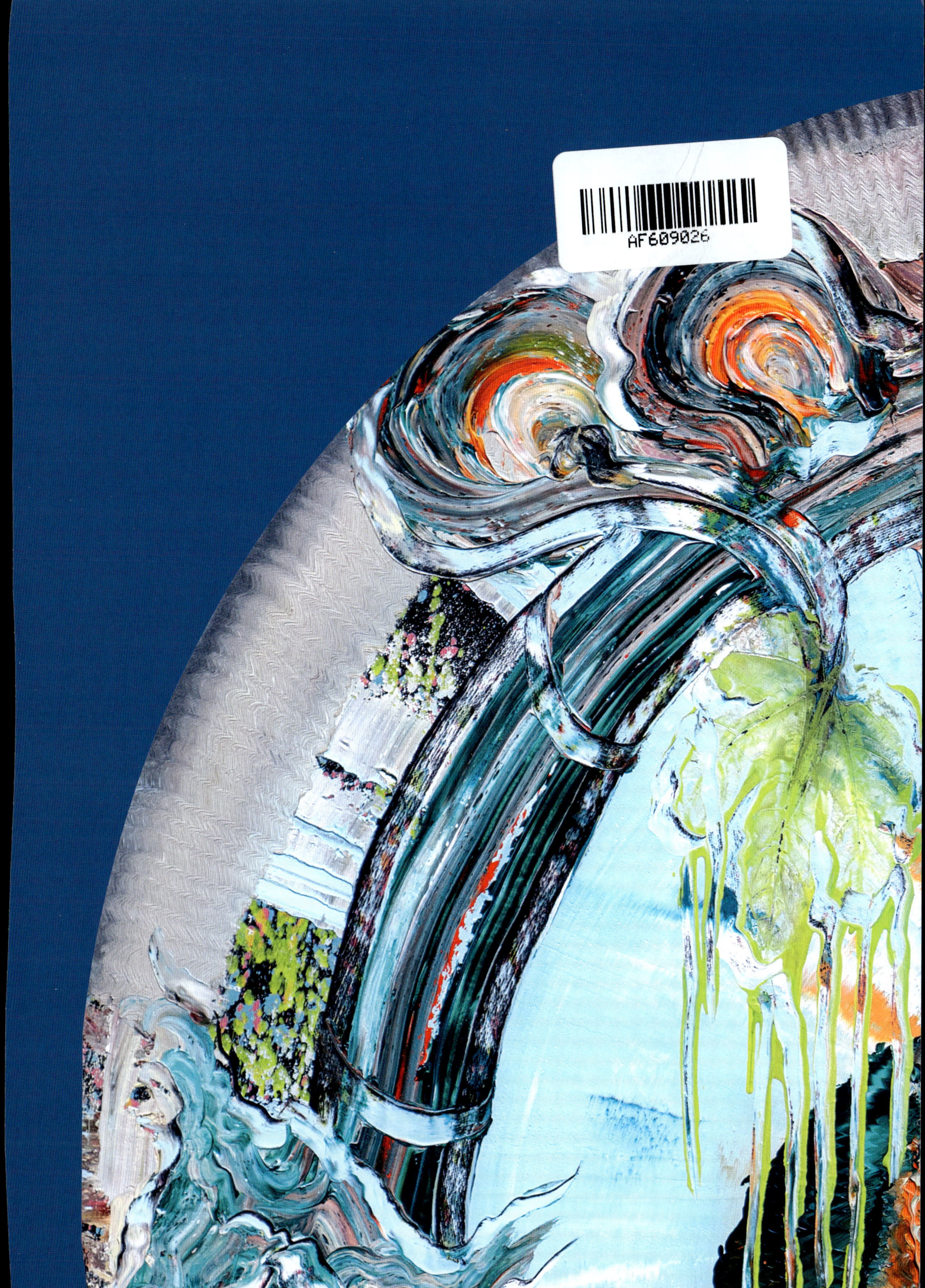

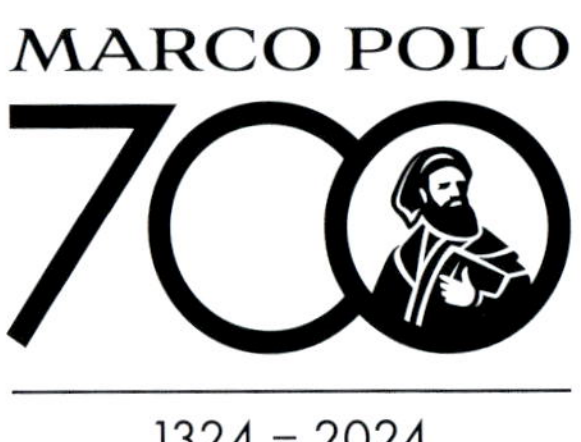
MARCO POLO
700
1324 – 2024

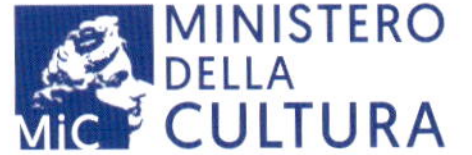
MiC
MINISTERO
DELLA
CULTURA

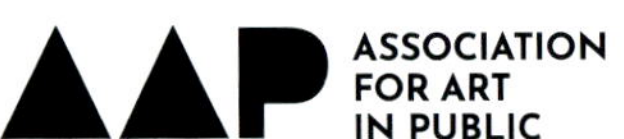
AAP
ASSOCIATION
FOR ART
IN PUBLIC

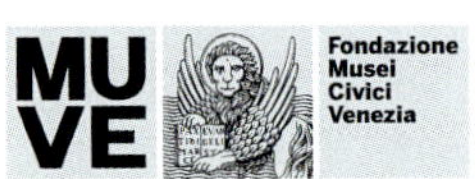
MU
VE
Fondazione
Musei
Civici
Venezia

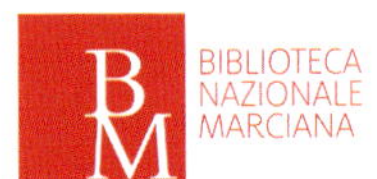
BM
BIBLIOTECA
NAZIONALE
MARCIANA

DIETMAR BRIXY

THE DESCRIPTION OF THE WORLD

BIBLIOTECA NAZIONALE MARCIANA
VENEZIA

24.8. – 22.9.2024

HIRMER

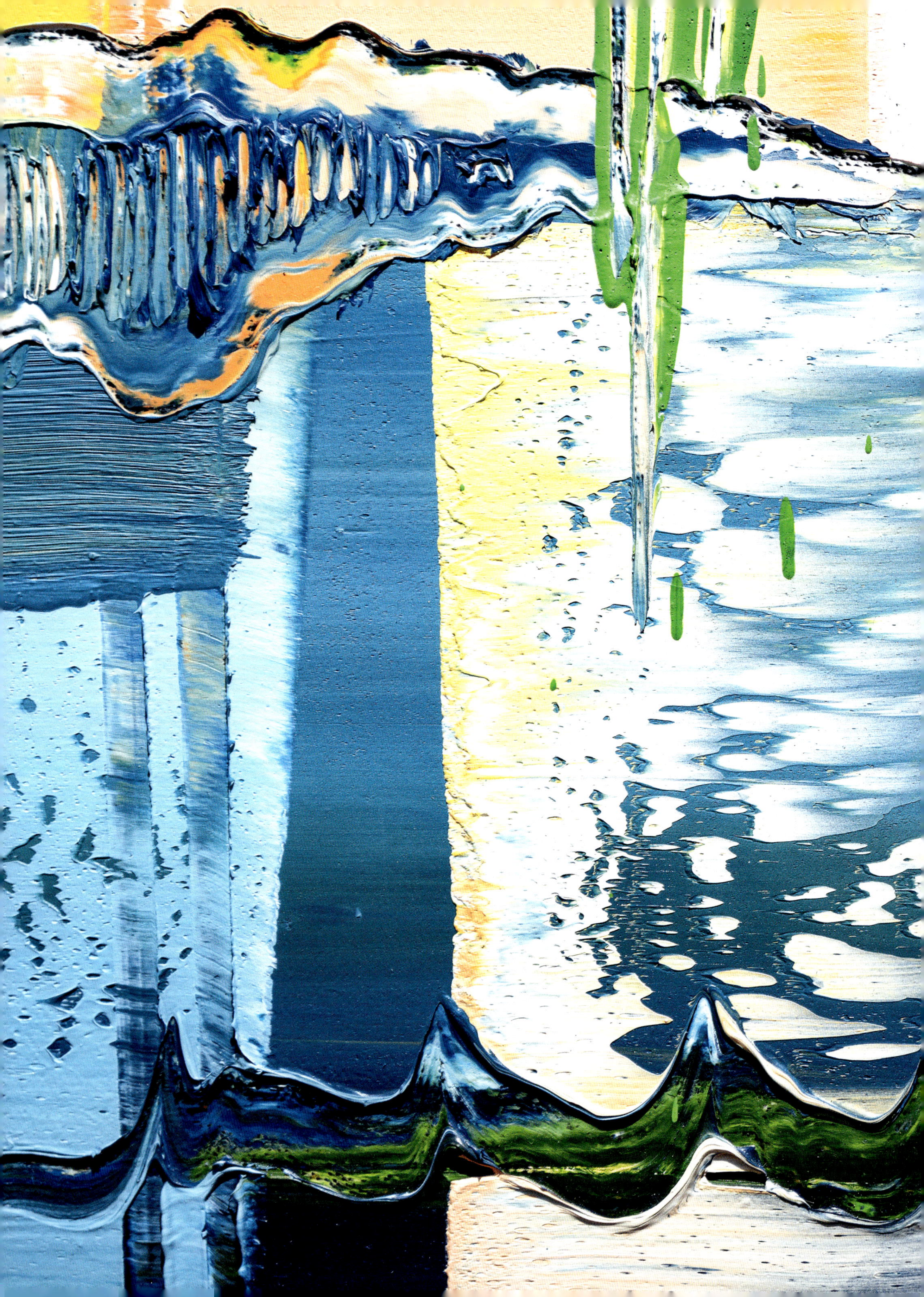

»WELTEN ENTSTEHEN –
WELTEN VERGEHEN.
EIN EWIGER KREISLAUF!
DEN KOSMOS BEGREIFEN –
ALS UNGREIFBAR.«

»WORLDS FORM –
WORLDS FADE.
AN ETERNAL CYCLE!
FATHOM THE WORLD –
AS BEING
UNFATHOMABLE.«

Dietmar Brixy

VORWORT

Dr. Stefano Trovato
Direktor, Biblioteca Nazionale Marciana

Venedig, 8. Februar 1438:
Aus Konstantinopel trifft eine Delegation ein, die von Kaiser Johannes VIII. persönlich angeführt wird. Im Gefolge befindet sich der Metropolit Bessarion aus der anatolischen Stadt Nicaea, der auf dem Konzil von Ferrara/Florenz zwischen 1438 und 1439 sowie später in der katholischen Kirche eine wichtige Rolle spielen sollte.

Es war der Beginn eines Weges, auf dem sich der byzantinische Prälat immer mehr in seine neue Heimat integrieren sollte. Zum Kardinal ernannt, stand er im Konklave nach der Katastrophe des Falls von Konstantinopel kurz vor seiner Wahl zum Papst. Doch er blieb auch der, der er vor 1438 gewesen war, so sehr, dass man ihn, mit einem glücklichen Ausdruck, „Inter Graecos Latinissimus, Inter Latinos Graecissimus" (der Griechischste unter den Latinern, der Latinischste unter den Griechen) nannte. Selbst in der Kunst seiner Zeit erschien Bessarion sowohl als „latinisch", wie in Federico da Montefeltros Studiolo, als auch griechisch, so in Piero della Francescas berühmter *Geißelung Christi*, wenn die jüngsten Interpretationen dieses faszinierenden Gemäldes zutreffen.

Das bis heute lebendige Zeichen seiner großartigen Persönlichkeit, seine berühmte Buchsammlung, die er, reich an griechischen und lateinischen Handschriften, am 26. Juni 1468 der Republik Venedig vermachte, blieb jahrzehntelang ohne feste Heimstatt. Ein angemessener Ort wurde erst nach einer erneuten Katastrophe (dem Sacco di Roma im Jahr 1527) errichtet, die einen weiteren wichtigen Protagonisten der Kulturgeschichte, Jacopo Sansovino, in den sicheren Hafen von Venedig brachte. Ihm verdanken wir das prachtvolle Gebäude der Bibliothek: die Libreria Sansoviniana.

Deren Innenraum, geschmückt mit einem großartigen Bildzyklus, dessen Bedeutung zum Nachdenken über die kommunikative Kraft der Kunst anregt, öffnet sich nun, wie schon seit Jahren, anlässlich der 60. Biennale Arte 2024 den Anregungen der zeitgenössischen Kunst. Dietmar Brixy zeigt mit einer vom aktuellen Biennale-Thema „Foreigners Everywhere" inspirierten Inszenierung die Ergebnisse seiner Recherchen über die ewige Bewegung und den permanenten Wandel des Lebens und der Vielfalt der Welt, und dies in dem Jahr, in dem sich der Todestag Marco Polos zum 700. Mal jährt.

Dieses Zusammentreffen mag den aufgeklärten Besucher dazu veranlassen, über die unergründlichen Tiefen der Geschichte und der Kunst in einer Institution nachzudenken, die diesem Mann, der einst als Fremder nach Venedig kam, so viel zu verdanken hat, und der sich, um es mit den Worten eines der griechischen Autoren der Bibliothek des Bessarion auszudrücken, als ein Geschenk an die Menschheit erwies:

„Aber wenn ein Mann von Natur aus begabt ist und darüber hinaus die Bildung durch unsere Literatur erhält, wird er tatsächlich zu einem Geschenk der Götter an die Menschheit, indem er das Licht der Erkenntnis entzündet, eine Art politischer Verfassung gründet, die Feinde seines Landes in die Flucht schlägt oder sogar weit über die Erde und das Meer reist und sich so als Mann von heldenhaftem Charakter erweist."

Biblioteca Nazionale Marciana

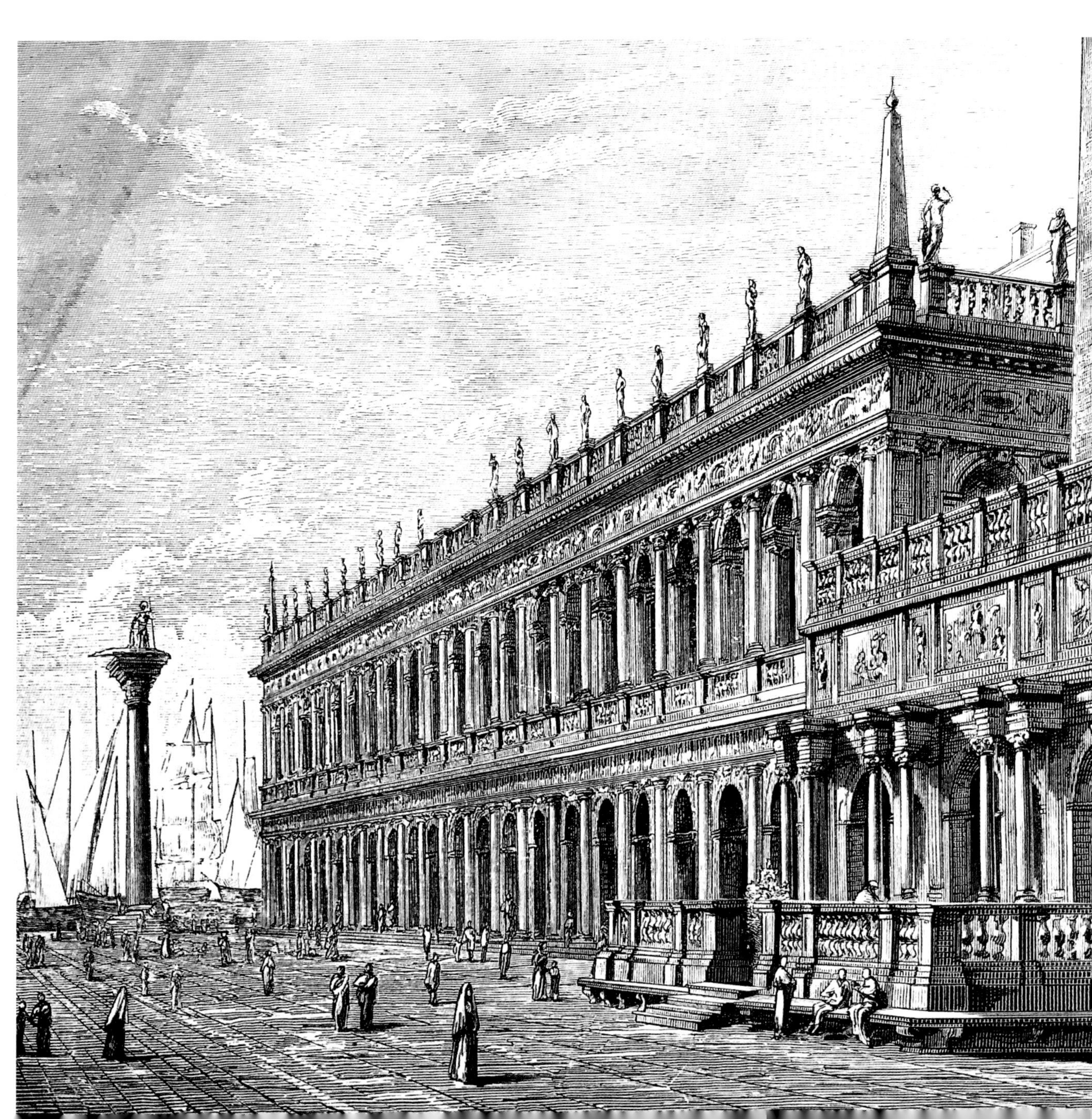

FOREWORD

Dr. Stefano Trovato
Director, Biblioteca Nazionale Marciana

Venice, February 8, 1438:
A delegation led by the emperor himself, John VIII, arrives from Constantinople. In the entourage there is Bessarion, the metropolitan of the Anatolian city of Nicaea, destined to play an important role in the Council of Florence, held between 1438 and 1439, and then in the Catholic Church.

It was the beginning of a journey that would witness the further integration of the Byzantine prelate in his new homeland: appointed cardinal, the conclave held after the catastrophe of the fall of Constantinople saw him very close to being elected pope. However, he stayed what he had also been before 1438, so much so that he was described as "Inter Graecos Latinissimus, Inter Latinos Graecissimus" ("the most Greek among the Latins, the most Latin among the Greeks"). Even in the art of his time Bessarion appeared both "Latin," as in Federico da Montefeltro's Studiolo, and Greek, as in Piero della Francesca's famous *Flagellation of Christ*, if recent interpretations of this fascinating painting are true.

To this day, his renowned library collection, rich in Greek and Latin manuscripts, which was donated to the Republic of Venice on June 26, 1468 is a living symbol of his splendid personality. This library collection remained for decades without a permanent home. A special venue was built only after a further catastrophe (the Sack of Rome in 1527), which brought another important protagonist of the history of culture to the secure refuge of Venice, Jacopo Sansovino, to whom we owe the splendid building of the Biblioteca, known as the Libreria Sansoviniana.

The interior, adorned with a fabulous pictorial cycle which leads us to ponder the communicative power of art, now opens, as it has for years, to the suggestions of contemporary art on the occasion of the 60th Biennale Arte 2024. With a production inspired by the current topic of this year's Biennale, "Foreigners Everywhere", Dietmar Brixy shows the results of his research on the eternal movement, the permanent change of life, and the diversity within the world, also coinciding with the 700th anniversary of Marco Polo's death.

This coincidence may lead the enlightened visitor to meditate on the impenetrable depth of history and art in an institution that owes a lot to someone who was once a foreigner to Venice and was then able to demonstrate being a gift to humanity – as described by one of the Greek authors in Bessarion's library:

"But when a man is naturally well endowed, and moreover receives the education of our literature, he becomes actually a gift of the gods to mankind, either by kindling the light of knowledge, or by founding some kind of political constitution, or by routing numbers of his country's foes, or even by travelling far over the earth and far by sea, and thus proving himself a man of heroic mould."

Biblioteca Nazionale Marciana, Sale di Lettura
Innenansicht / Inside view

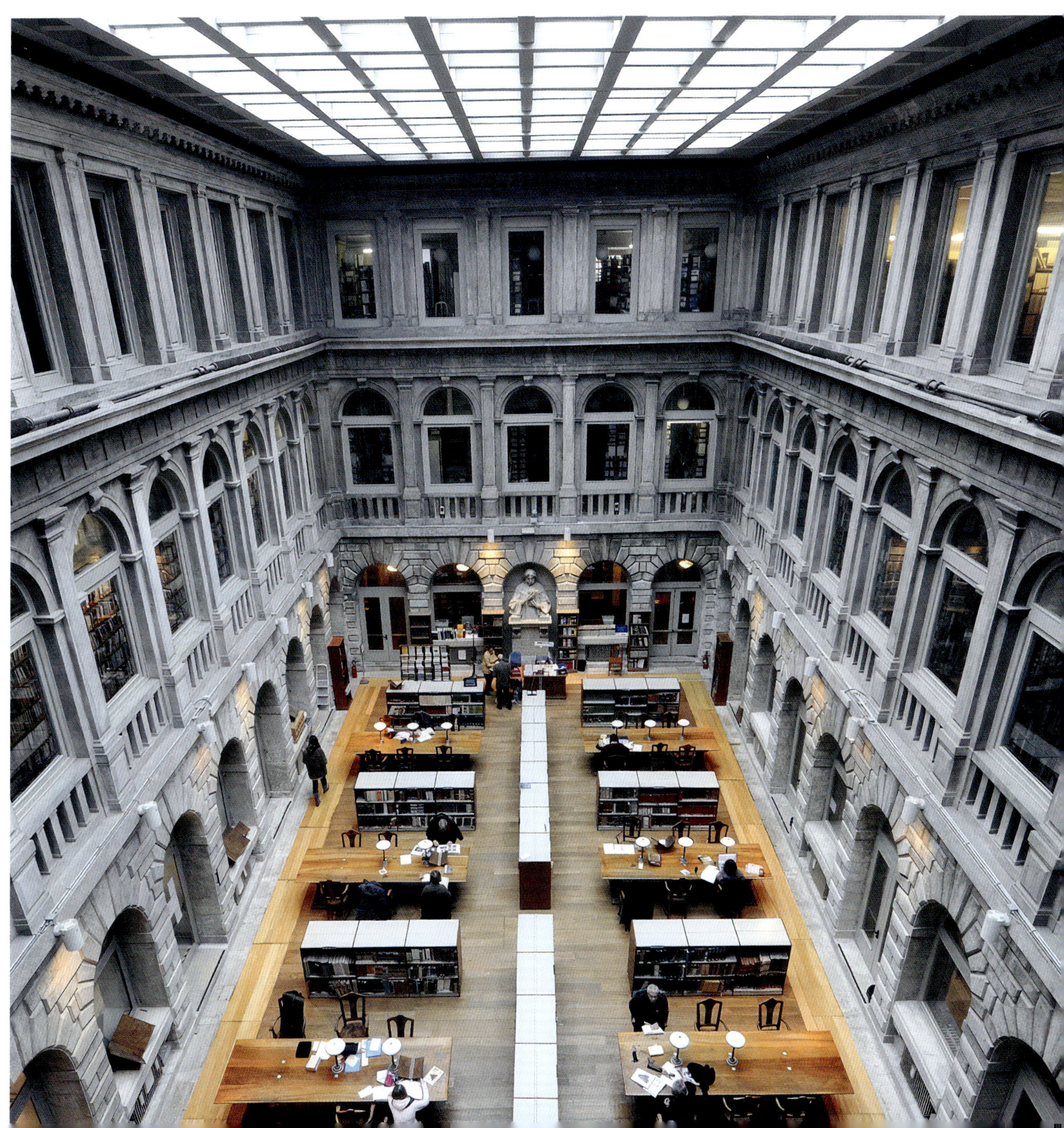

EINLEITUNG

Dirk Geuer
Chefkurator der Ausstellungsserie „At Home Abroad"
Biblioteca Nazionale Marciana

Venedig ist seit dem Mittelalter das Tor zur Welt. Von hier aus brachen Entdecker in noch unbekannte Regionen der Erde auf, um sie zu erforschen und bedeutende Handelsrouten aufzubauen. Über die Jahrhunderte kamen viele als Fremde in die Serenissima und wurden hier heimisch – ein Prozess, der sich bis heute fortsetzt. So wurde die Lagunenstadt zu einem Schmelztiegel der Nationen und Kulturen.

Eine zentrale und geradezu symbolische Figur in diesem Prozess ist Marco Polo. Aus einer angesehenen venezianischen Händlerfamilie stammend, brach er 1271 in den Fernen Osten auf und kehrte erst 24 Jahre später nach Venedig zurück. Seine Erzählungen fanden ihre Niederschrift in dem Buch *Il Milione*, auch bekannt als „Description of the World" (Beschreibung der Welt), verfasst von Rustichello da Pisa. Der Titel dieser Schrift gibt der Ausstellung mit Dietmar Brixy ihren Namen. Wie Marco Polo einst seine Leser, lädt Brixy den Betrachter ein, sich mit ihm auf eine Reise zu begeben und die Welt als einen Ort der Begegnung, der Offenheit und des Miteinanders zu begreifen. Hier schlägt er nicht nur die Brücke zur diesjährigen Biennale unter dem Motto „Foreigners Everywhere", sondern auch zum Projekt „At Home Abroad", einer Serie von vier Ausstellungen internationaler zeitgenössischer Künstler im Salone Sansoviniano der Biblioteca Nazionale Marciana, die das „Fremdsein" auf vielfältige Weise thematisieren.

Die Faszination für das Unbekannte, das Fernweh und der Wunsch, die Welt zu entdecken, sind seit jeher zentrale Themen in der Kunst. Künstler haben sich immer wieder von Reisen und der Begegnung mit der Vielfalt fremder Kulturen inspirieren lassen. Auch Dietmar Brixy ist ein solcher Reisender, ein Suchender. Seine Expeditionen führten ihn in verschiedene europäische Länder, aber auch nach Malaysia, Mexiko, Indien, Bali, die Seychellen und die USA. Über die Jahre hat er einen eigenen und unverwechselbaren Ansatz entwickelt, seine Erfahrungen, Erlebnisse und Wahrnehmungen in seinen Werken zu verarbeiten.

Rechts / right:
Journey, 2023
240 × 180 cm

Seine expressiven Kompositionen werden von lebendigen Farben bestimmt, die er in einem zwischen meditativer Ruhe und schwungvoller Dynamik variierenden Prozess mit Pinseln, Spachteln, Kämmen und bloßen Händen auf die Leinwand aufträgt. Die vielschichtigen Strukturen, Farbfelder und Formen wirken in ihrer Gesamtheit wie ein Kaleidoskop und eröffnen dem Betrachter eine Welt, die sowohl fremd als auch vertraut erscheint. Es ist, als

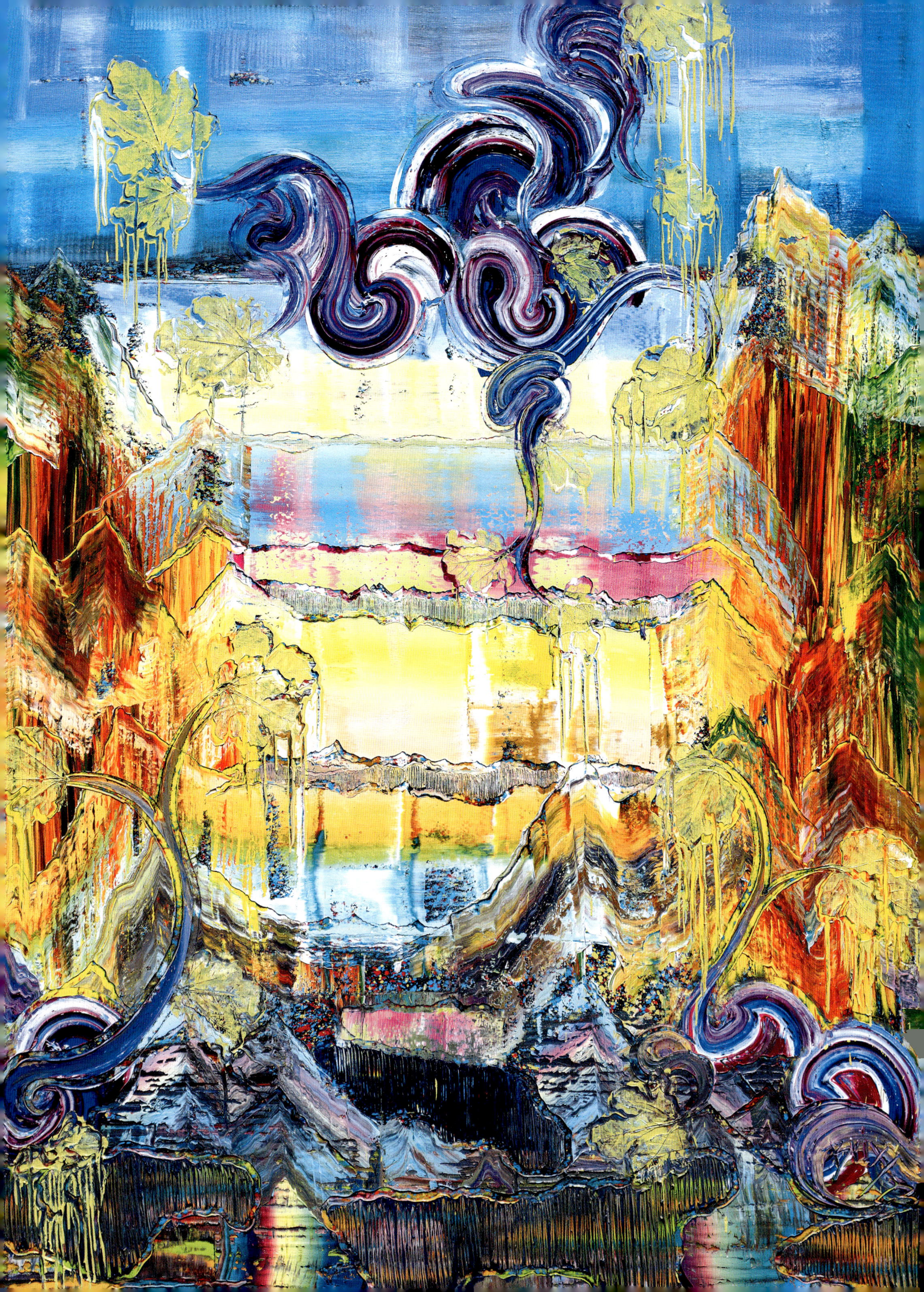

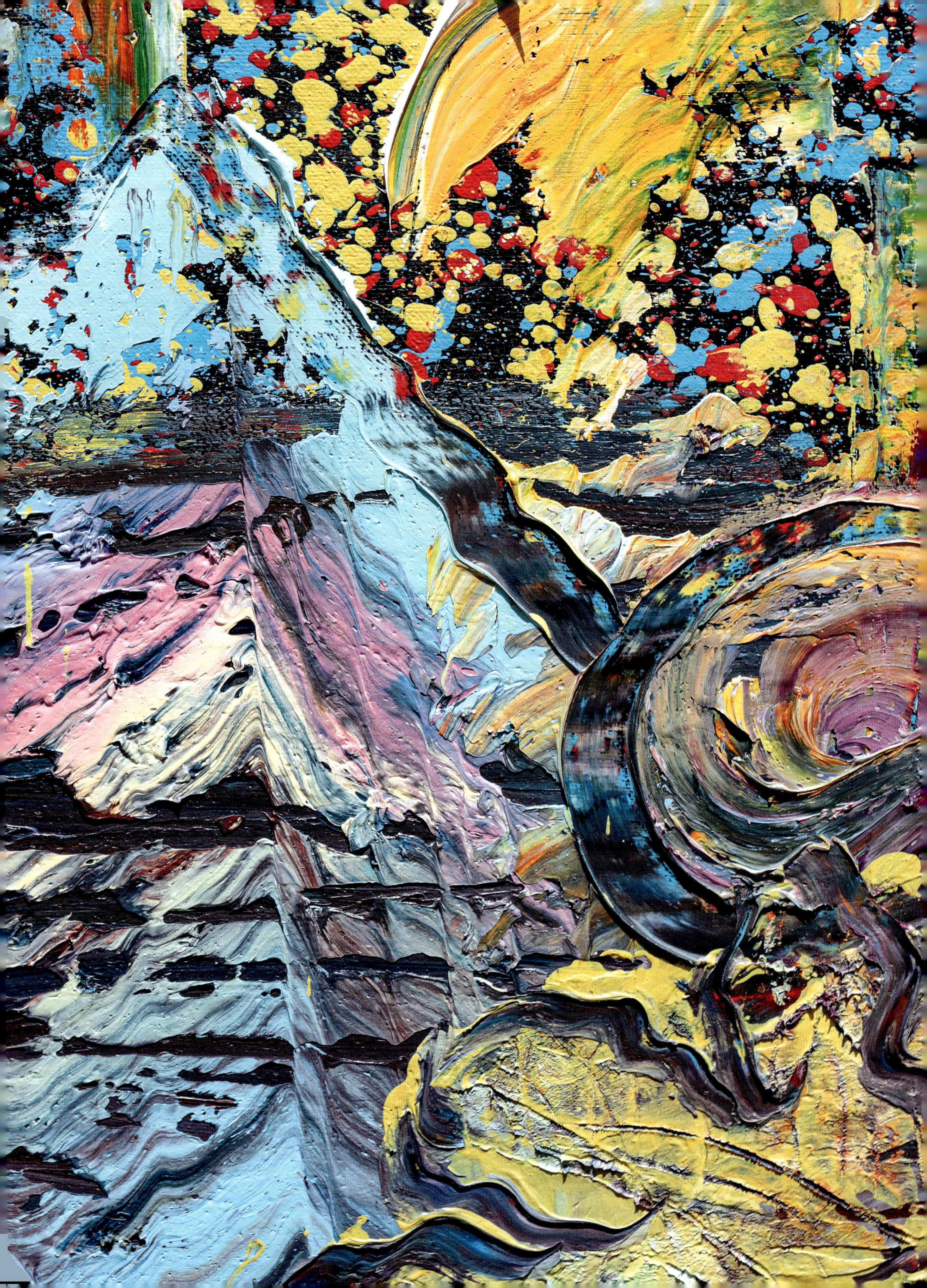

könne Brixy die Grenzen der Realität durchbrechen. Schicht für Schicht zieht er uns tiefer in seine Kompositionen hinein. Wie ein Vorhang geben ornamentale Formen den Blick frei auf ein zartes, flirrendes Zentrum, in dem phantastische Landschaften unseren Blick einfangen.

Seine Inspiration findet der Künstler in der Natur, sei es in seinem paradiesischen Garten in Mannheim oder in entfernten Regionen der Welt. So entdeckte er auf der Kanareninsel La Palma für sich das dort allgegenwärtige Feigenblatt, das seitdem als wiederkehrendes Motiv in seinen Bildern vorkommt. Die markanten Elemente verbinden als gegenständliches Motiv die Wirklichkeit mit der abstrakten Landschaft.

Eine Besonderheit im Œuvre Dietmar Brixys sind seine Tondi, die *Bamboo Bubbles*. Wie ein Globus, der die Kontinente, Ozeane und den Verlauf der Erdrotation zeigt, illustrieren die kreisrunden Bilder die ewige Bewegung und den permanenten Wandel des Lebens. Sie stehen sinnbildlich für das Werden und Vergehen der Natur, für ihre Zyklen und Kreisläufe, aber auch für die Vielfalt der Welt und die Diversität von Kulturen und Identitäten, die in einer harmonischen Collage zusammenfließen. Der Künstler fängt die Essenz des Universums ein und bringt sie in Form von leuchtenden Farbexplosionen und natürlichen Chiffren auf der Leinwand zum Ausdruck. Mit der drei Meter hohen Installation *Endless Journey*, die speziell für die Ausstellung in Venedig entstanden ist, überführt Dietmar Brixy sein malerisches Werk erstmals in die dritte Dimension. Auf acht Bildtafeln entzündet er in einem großen, umschreitbaren Panorama ein wahres Feuerwerk an Farben und Formen und ermöglicht dem Besucher ein gänzlich neues räumliches Erleben seiner Kunst. Der oktogonale Grundriss greift die Form und Dimension des sich darüber befindenden Gemäldes von Tizian auf und tritt damit in einen Dialog mit seiner historischen Umgebung.

Doch auch in anderer Form stellen Brixys Arbeiten einen engen Bezug zum Ort der Ausstellung her, den Sale Monumentali der ehrwürdigen Biblioteca Marciana. Unter den Augen von Tizians *La Sapienza* und Veroneses Philosophen legen antike Landkarten und Globen Zeugnis ab von der Neugier des Menschen und seinem fortwährenden Bestreben, die Welt zu erkunden und zu kartografieren, immer auf der Suche nach Erkenntnis. Heute ist die Erde bis in beinahe jeden Winkel erforscht. Und doch bleiben Fragen offen. Schon Marco Polo soll gesagt haben: „Ich habe nicht die Hälfte von dem erzählt, was ich gesehen habe, weil keiner mir geglaubt hätte." Hier setzt Dietmar Brixy an. Er zeigt uns eine andere, innere Welt voller Wunder, die zu erkunden uns selbst obliegt. Mit den Augen eines Entdeckenden durchstreifen wir seine Landschaften und tauchen ein in die unendlichen Dimensionen menschlicher Vorstellungskraft.

Links / left:
Journey, 2023
240 × 180 cm, Detail

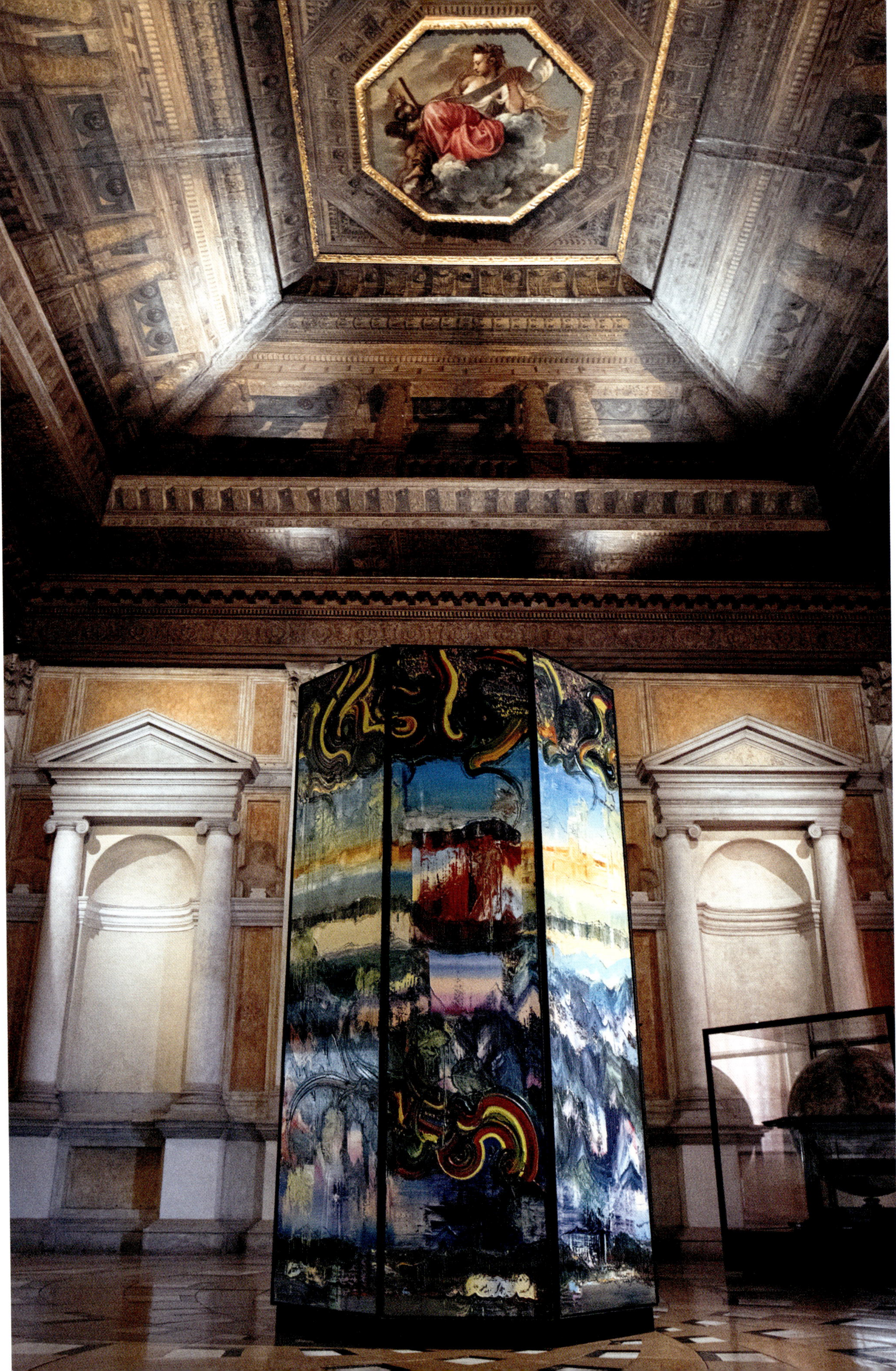

INTRODUCTION

Dirk Geuer
Chief Curator for the exhibition series “At Home Abroad”
Biblioteca Nazionale Marciana

Venice has been the portal to the world since medieval times. From here, explorers started off to unknown regions of the world in order to discover them and build important commercial routes. Over the decades many came to the Serenissima and became natives, a process which is ongoing to this day. This is how the lagune city turned into a melting pot of nations and cultures.

A central and symbolic figure in this process is Marco Polo. Coming from a renowned Venetian family of salesmen, he started off to the Far East in 1271 and returned to Venice only 24 years later. His tales were collected in the book *Il Milione*, also known under the title *The Description of the World* written by Rustichello da Pisa. The name for the art exhibition with Dietmar Brixy comes from the title of this text. Like Marco Polo, Dietmar Brixy invites the viewer to follow him on a journey and to perceive the world as a place of encounter, openness, and togetherness. With this, not only does he connect to this year’s motto of the Biennale “Foreigners Everywhere”, but also to the project “At Home Abroad”, a series of four art exhibitions by international contemporary artists in the Salone Sansoviniano of the Biblioteca Nazionale Marciana that deal with being a foreigner in various ways.

The fascination for the unknown, wanderlust, and the desire to discover the world have always been relevant topics in art. Artists have always been inspired by travels and the encounter with the variety of foreign cultures. Dietmar Brixy is also such a traveler, a seeker. His expeditions took him to various European countries, but also to Malaysia, Mexico, India, Bali, the Seychelles and the USA. Over the years, he has developed his own unique approach to processing his experiences and perceptions in his works.

His expressive compositions are determined by lively colors, which he applies to the canvas with brushes, spatulas, combs, and bare hands in a process that varies between meditative calm and energetic dynamics. The multitude of structures, color fields and forms, viewed as a whole, act like a kaleidoscope and immerse the viewer in a world that simultaneously appears both strange and familiar. It's like Brixy is breaking the boundaries of reality. Layer by layer, he draws the viewer deeper into his compositions. Like a curtain, ornamental silhouettes reveal an elegant, shimmering center in which fantastical landscapes capture our gaze.

Links / left:
Endless Journey, 2024
Oktogon, 8 Tafeln, je /
Octagon, 8 boards,
each 300 × 70 cm
S. / p. 17: Detail

The artist finds his inspiration in nature, be it in his empyrean garden in Mannheim or in distant lands of the world. This is how Brixy discovered for himself the omnipresent fig leaf on the Canary Islands La Palma, an object which ever since is a recurrent motif in his paintings. The distinctive elements combine reality with the fictional landscape as a representational motif.

A special feature of Dietmar Brixy's œuvre are his tondi, the so-called *Bamboo Bubbles*. Like a globe that shows the continents, the oceans, and the movement of Earth's rotation, the circular images symbolize the eternal movement and constant change of life. They illustrate the cycle of growth and decay in nature, but also the diversity within the world and the multiplicity of cultures and identities that together flow in a harmonious collage. The artist captures the essence of the universe and expresses it on canvas in the form of bright explosions of color and natural ciphers.

With the three-meter tall installation *Endless Journey*, which has specifically been created for the art exhibition in Venice, Dietmar Brixy translates his picturesque works into three dimensions for the first time. Within a big, circumnavigable panorama of eight canvases, the artist lights a real firework of colors and forms and allows the viewer to explore a new spatial experience of his art. Its octagonal outline picks the form and dimension of the above-situated painting by Titian and hereby enters in a dialog with its historical surroundings.

But there are also other ways in which Brixy's works closely interact with the place of the exhibition – the Sale Monumentali of the honorable Biblioteca Marciana. Under the eyes of Titian's *La Sapienza* and Veronese's philosophers, ancient maps and globes give evidence of the curiosity of humanity and its constant desire to discover the world, always on the search for insight. Today, nearly every corner of the world has been explored. And yet many questions remain unanswered. Marco Polo is already said to have stated the following: "I have not even told half of what I have seen because no one would have believed me." This is what Dietmar Brixy ties to. He shows us a different, inner world full of wonders, of which discovery is our own responsibility. With the eyes of the explorer, we roam through his landscapes and dive into the endless dimensions of human imagination.

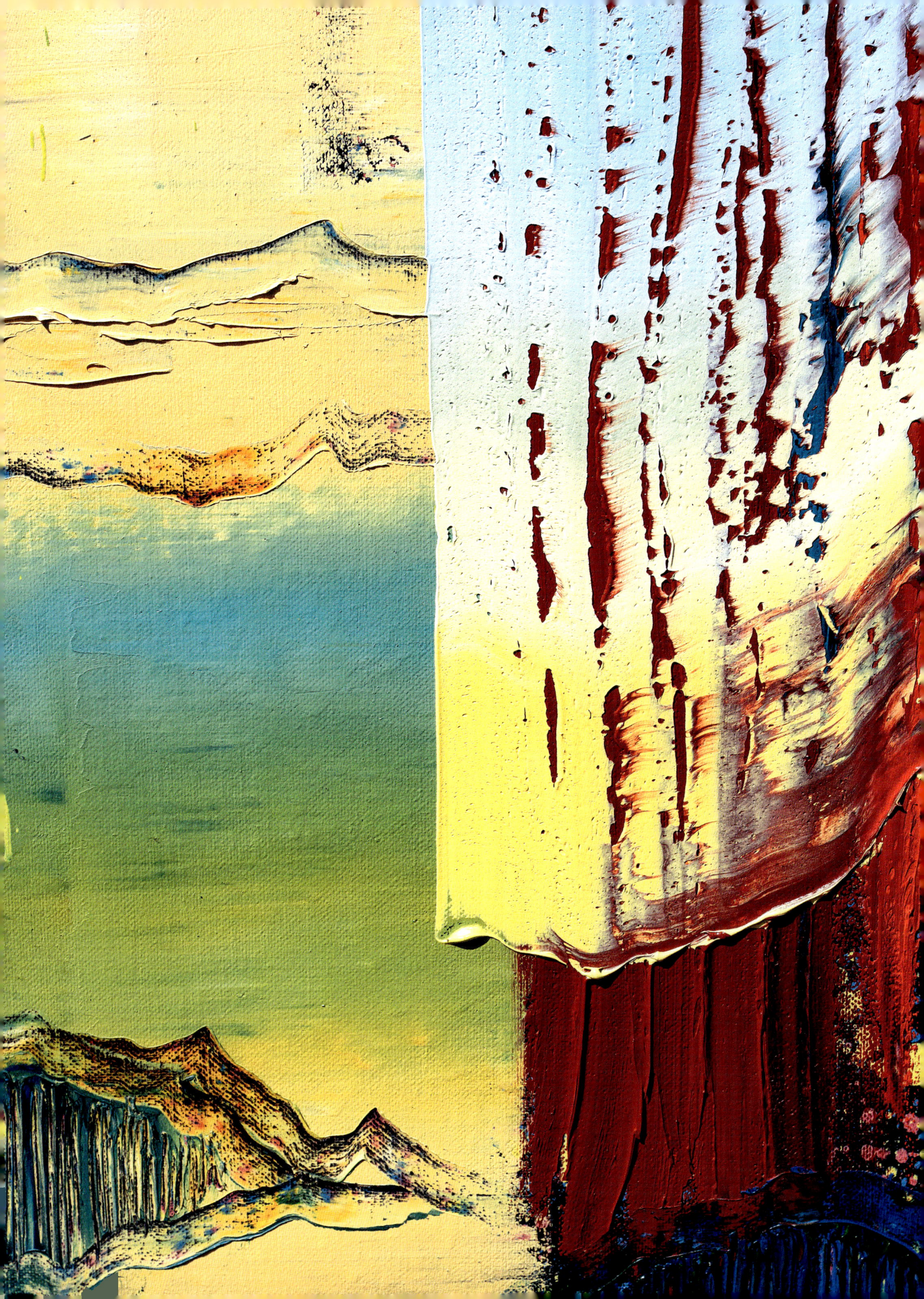

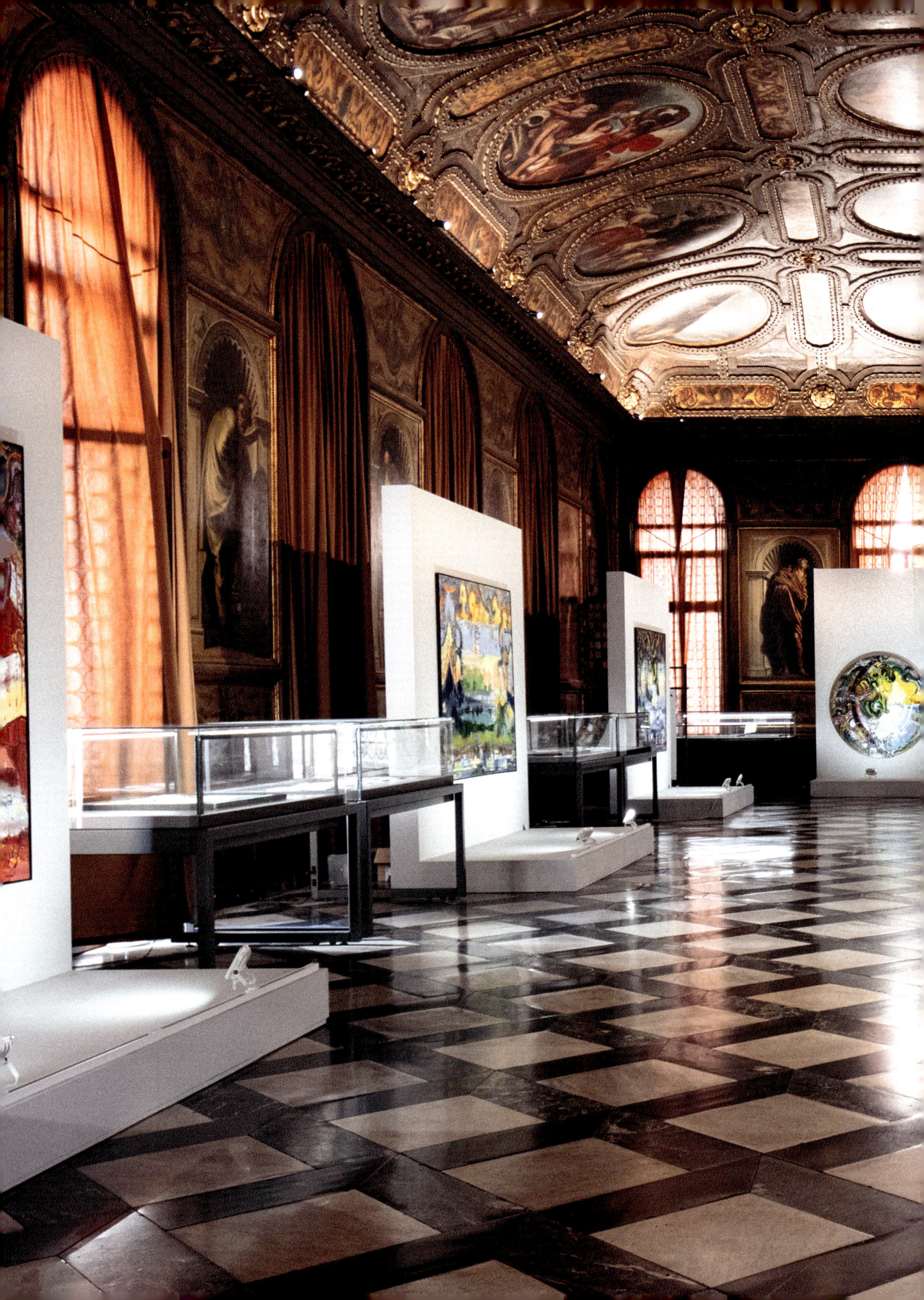

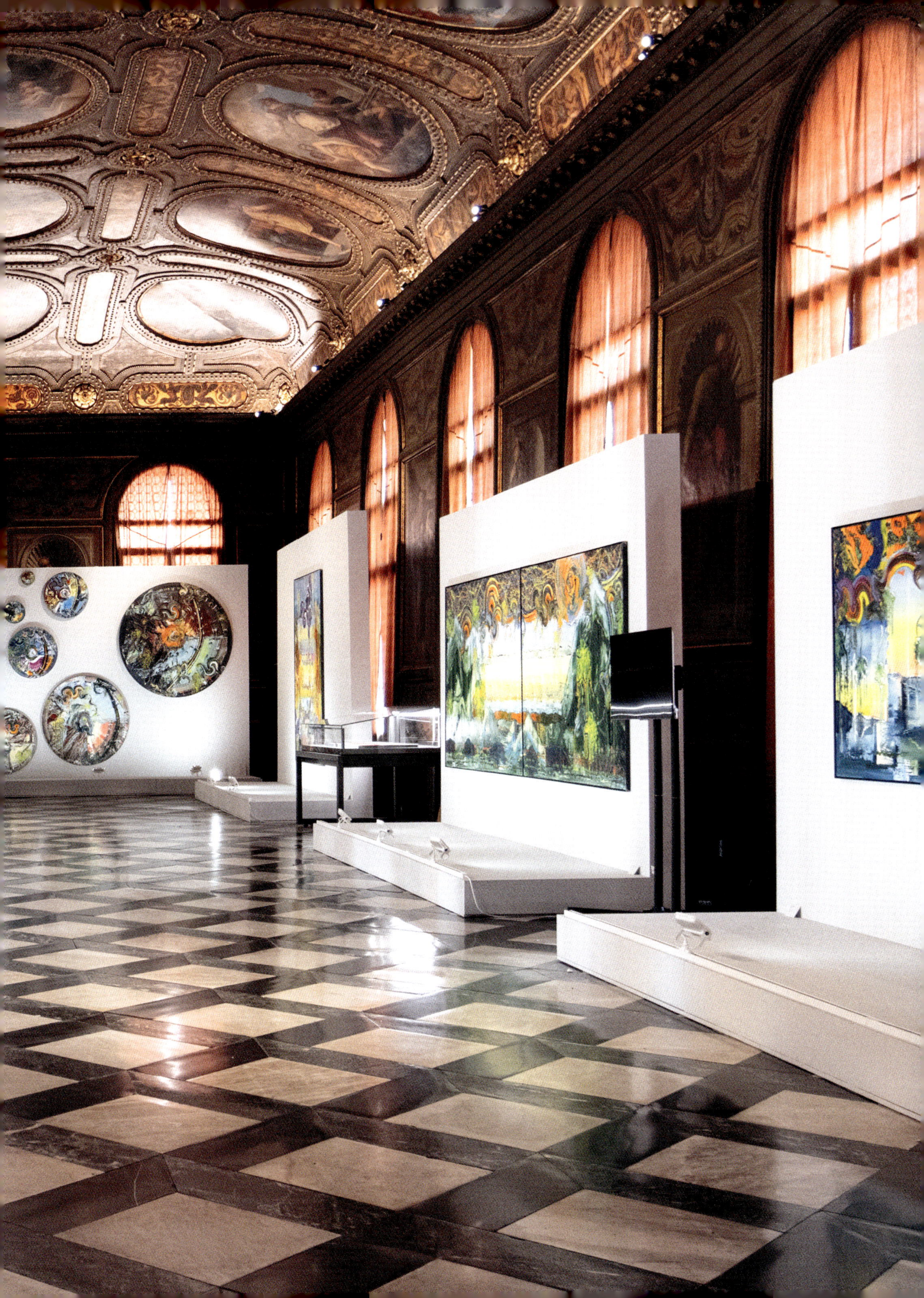

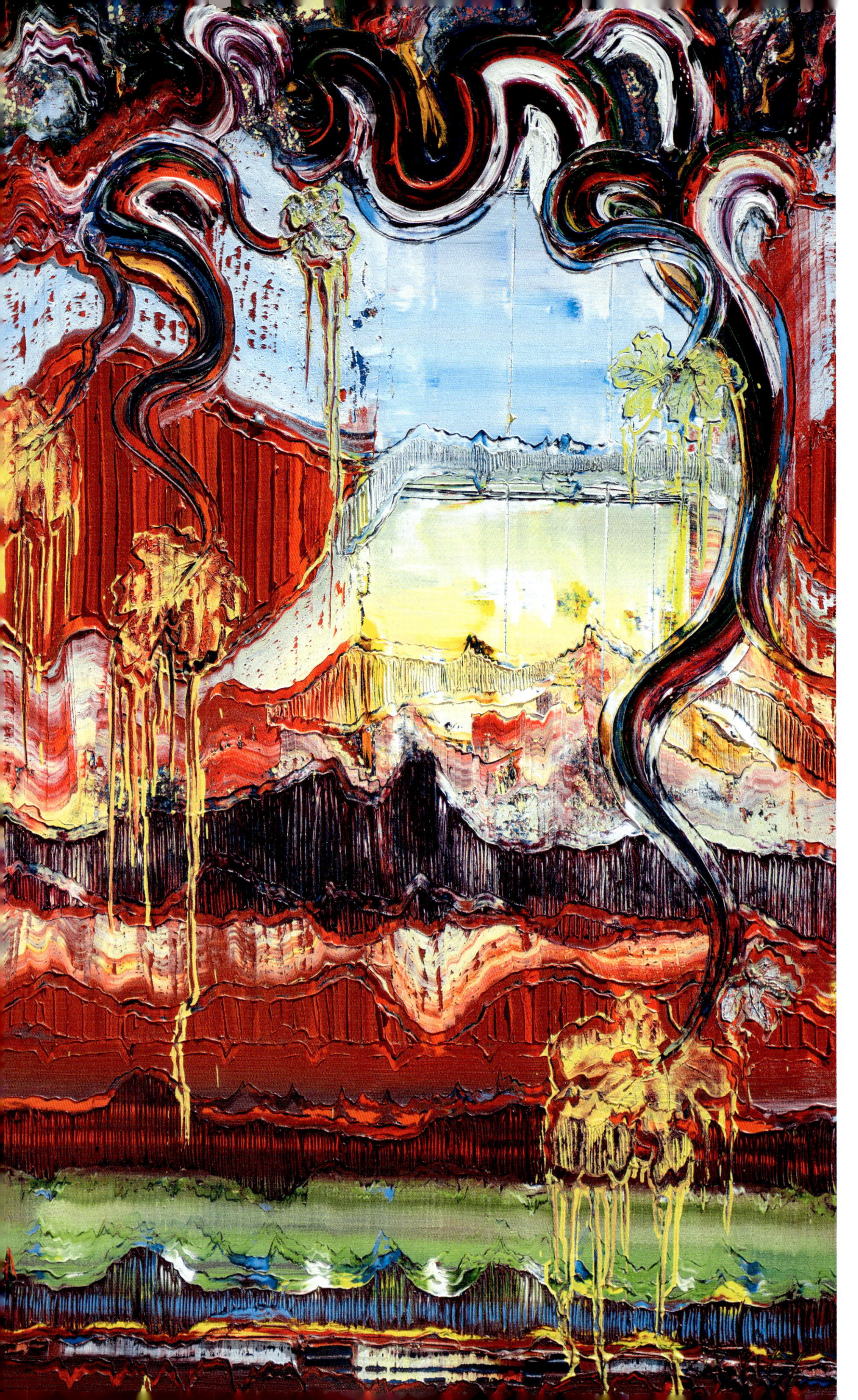

DIETMAR BRIXY
CONNECTED

Dr. Tayfun Belgin

„Dieses Werk, von dem hier zu reden ist, ist gewachsen seit Jahren und wächst an jedem Tage wie ein Wald und verliert keine Stunde.“[1]

Und die Kunst von Dietmar Brixy schreitet voran, jeden Tag, in einfühlsamer Ästhetik, die nicht frei ist von innerer Spannung und in einem wunderbaren Umfeld zur Welt kommt. Die Arbeiten entstehen in einer Kunstwelt, die im Inneren immer wieder auf sich selbst verweist und im Äußeren eng umfasst ist von Natur und ihrem koloristischen Reichtum: von Bäumen, Pflanzen, Sträuchern und vielfältigen Blumenarten. Ein Repertoire, das die Begeisterung des Großstädters für die Natur versinnbildlicht.

Der Maler, Zeichner, Plastiker Dietmar Brixy hat sich mit dem Erwerb des ehemaligen Pumpwerks in Mannheim-Neckarau ein Atelierparadies geschaffen, in das er immer wieder Interessierte einlädt. Hier begegnet uns ein Begeisterter der Natur, der sich ihr vornehmlich in seinen opulenten Gemälden annähert, um sich dann doch wieder leise zu verabschieden – bis zum nächsten Bild. Doch handelt es sich wirklich um die Darstellung von Natur? Verfallen wir nicht einer wunderbaren Illusion, wenn wir unsere Augen, unseren Geist derart rational beeinflussen? Beantworten wir diese Frage zunächst mit dem Symbolisten Maurice Denis, Mitbegründer der Künstlergruppe Nabis, Maler und auch Theoretiker, der 1890 sein Publikum in der Zeitschrift *Art et Critique* wissen ließ:

„Sich ins Gedächtnis rufen: Ein Bild ist – bevor es ein Schlachtpferd, eine nackte Frau oder irgendeine Anekdote darstellt – vor allen Dingen eine plane Fläche, die in einer bestimmten Ordnung mit Farben bedeckt ist.“[2]

Ein folgenreicher Satz für die Moderne – mit quasi ewiger Gültigkeit. Kein Appell, nur noch abstrakt zu malen, so weit war man damals ja noch nicht, sondern sich auf das zu besinnen, was (damals) ein Bild ausmachte: eine Malerei, die sich ihrer Stilmittel bewusst ist und nicht bloß Außerbildliches repräsentiert. Denis’ Einsicht ist wesentlich für die moderne Malerei. Das Bild wurde nicht gemordet, seine Rolle sollte sich verändern. Die Maler waren sich bewusst, dass die damals schon sehr sichtbare Momentfotografie ihnen auf den Fersen war. So gewinnt auch der berühmte Ausspruch Vincent van Goghs: „Aber der Maler der Zukunft ist ein Kolorist“[3] in diesem Zusammenhang an Bedeutung. Zwar formulierte dies van Gogh für sich und seine eigene Kunst, allerdings ist auch diese Einsicht fundamental. Und weiter: Als Erster im 20. Jahrhundert ließ uns Paul Klee auf seiner Tunisreise am 16. April 1914

Links / left:
Reflect, 2021
160 × 100 cm

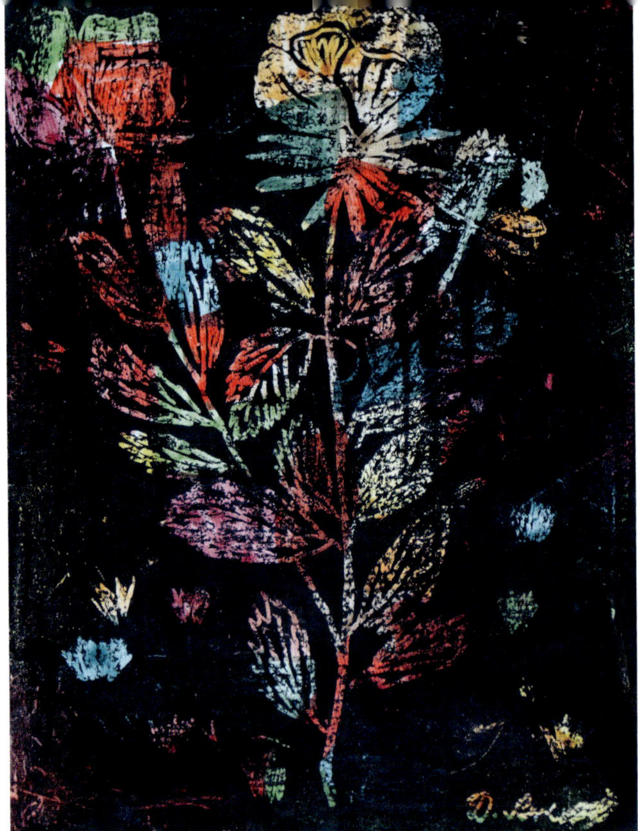

Ohne Titel / Untitled, 1968
Wachsmalstift auf Papier /
wax crayon on paper
28 × 21 cm

über einen Tagebucheintrag in Kairouan wissen: „Die Farbe hat mich. Ich brauche nicht nach ihr zu haschen. Sie hat mich für immer, ich weiß das. Das ist der glücklichen Stunde Sinn: Ich und die Farbe sind eins. Ich bin Maler."[4]

Brixys Malerei der frühen Jahre, also vor dem Umzug 2003 in das heute umschwärmte ehemalige Pumpwerk, war gekennzeichnet von einem gänzlich anderen Temperament als seine heutigen, farbanmutigen Werke. Farbe war für ihn zweifelsohne das bestimmende Mittel, um sich bildnerisch auszudrücken. Die damals schon eingeleitete Technik der Setzung und späteren Entfernung von Farbschichten wurde im Laufe der Jahre in beeindruckender Manier weiterentwickelt und bestimmt die heutige polyvalente Koloristik, die viele Sammler begeistert. Im Gespräch lässt Dietmar Brixy den Fragenden jedoch auch wissen, dass er diese Technik schon als Kind beherrschte, und verweist gerne auf kleine Werke aus seiner Kindheit.

In den Werken der 1990er-Jahre sehen wir in aller Regel einen vielschichtigen Dialog von Farben und Formen. Farbe dient hier nahezu durchgehend als Matrix für die aktionistisch eingesetzten, durchsichtigen Formen, die in ihren Umrissen an Menschen erinnern, aber auch an gerade noch erkennbare Naturformen wie Schneckenhäuser, Pflanzen und Bäume. Vieles erscheint gleichsam hingehaucht, der Auflösung nahe oder kurz vor einer Umwandlung in abstrakte Zeichen. Mit viel Phantasie lassen sich einige dieser zumeist androgynen Formen auch als im Bildraum schwebende Krieger mit Schild deuten. Mal sind sie um eine Leiter versammelt, mal rauschen sie durch das Bildgeviert, mal schwimmen sie regelrecht in den Bildraum hinein.

Rechts / right:
Altes Pumpwerk
Mannheim-Neckarau

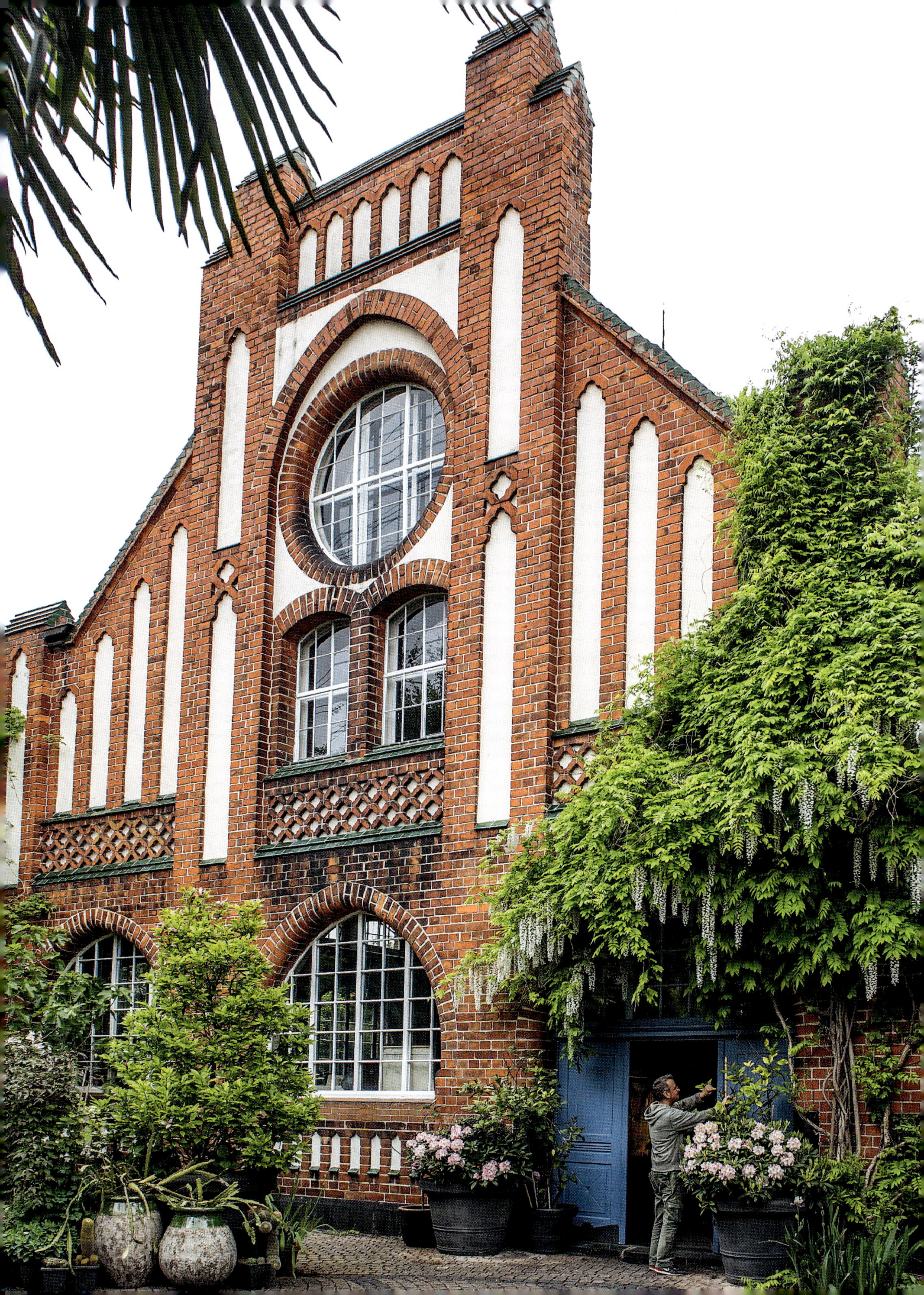

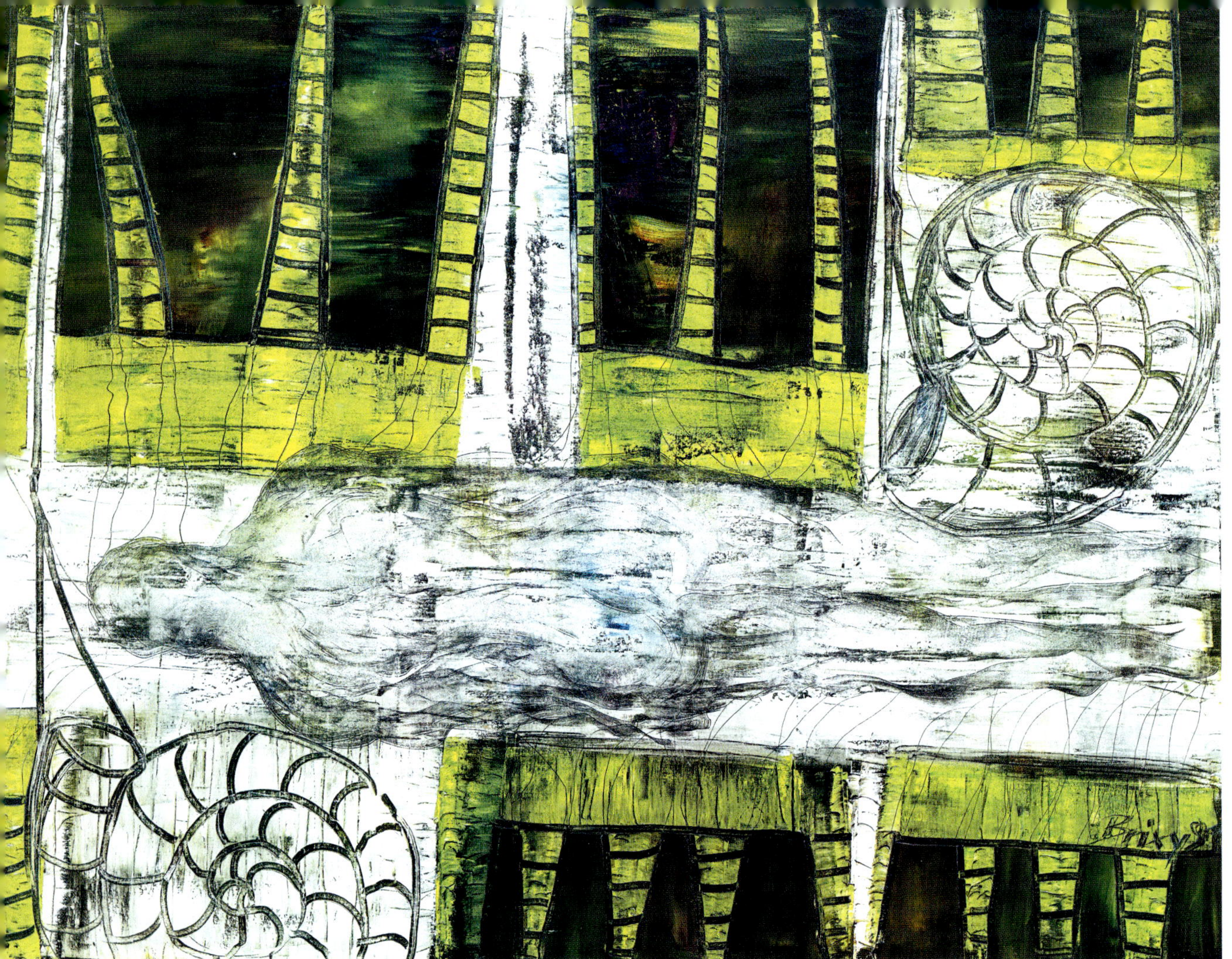

Ohne Titel / Untitled,
1991
240 × 180 cm

Bei diesen energetischen Bildern wird eine kategoriale Bestimmung der Kunst von Dietmar Brixy anschaulich. Der Maler bevorzugt eine Strategie des Andeutens, des In-die-Welt-Setzens von Formen und Figuren, deren Eindeutigkeit allerdings ein Geheimnis bleiben soll. Zu Anfang wurden die Werke noch betitelt, etwa *Schwimmer*, *Versunken*, *Dschungelwesen* oder *Gefunden*, und verweisen damit auf eine Daseinswelt, auch wenn diese in hoher Abstraktion in Szene gesetzt ist. In dieser Welt der erscheinenden und sich entfernenden Formen müssen sich die Betrachtenden ihr eigenes Bild machen. Eine Eindeutigkeit wird – bei allem malerischen Raffinement – strategisch verweigert. Ein Horizont ist nicht wahrzunehmen. Der Bezug von Horizontalität und Vertikalität, unser existenzieller Daseinsbezug, wird zugunsten einer kreativen, zugleich auch unordentlichen Bildwelt aufgegeben.

Diese Bildräume sind bis zum Bersten mit Farben und Formen angereichert. Es sind prozessartige Werke, die in einer inhaltlich bestimmten Logik aufeinander zu folgen scheinen. Brixy deutet ein Bildgeschehen an, ohne sich eindeutig positionieren zu wollen. Der temperamentvolle Bildraum scheint sich einem Chaos unterzuordnen, wobei dieser Terminus nicht so verstanden werden darf wie in der griechischen Antike, als lichtloser Schlund der Unterwelt, sondern neuzeitlich erfasst. Hier sind es Bildräume mit potenziellen Energien, quasi Vorboten einer universellen Ordnung. Brixy durchspielt in seinen Bildern die Gegensätze von Chaos und Ordnung. Beides ist evident und bestimmt somit die Bildstrategie dieser Zeit.

Um es mit Nietzsche auch positiv zu fassen; Zarathustra wendet sich zu Anfang seiner Tätigkeit verkündend an das Volk: „Ich sage euch: man muß noch Chaos in sich haben, um einen tanzenden Stern gebären zu können."[5]

Szenenwechsel: Der Vorhang geht auf. Dietmar Brixys Bildwelt hat sich nach 2015 in einer Weise transformiert, die uns erstaunen lässt. Wir werden Bildräumen ansichtig, die eine Radikalität offenbaren, die nicht vorhersehbar war. Brixy eröffnet uns ein Bildgeschehen, das wir von einer Art Bühne aus wahrnehmen. Er nimmt uns gleichsam an die Hand und führt uns in ein panoramatisches Bildgeschehen. Wir schauen von links nach rechts, von oben nach unten, halten uns kurz in der Mitte auf, um an einem Standort innezuhalten. Diese gewaltige Farbrhythmik, diese der Natur und ihren unendlichen Erscheinungen entnommene Koloristik, lassen uns zunächst einmal sprachlos.

„Cézanne, einmal gebeten zu beschreiben, was er unter ‚Motiv' verstünde, führte ‚sehr langsam' die gespreizten Finger beider Hände gegeneinander, faltete sie und verschränkte sie. Als ich davon las, erinnerte ich mich wieder, daß ich beim Anblick des Bildes die Kiefern und Felsblöcke als verschlungene Schriftzeichen gesehen hatte, so eindeutig wie unbestimmbar. – In einem Brief Cézannes las ich weiter, er male keinesfalls ‚nach der Natur' – seine Bilder seien vielmehr ‚Konstruktionen und Harmonien parallel zur Natur'."[6]

Sprachlich sensibel interpretiert Peter Handke die Werke seines Protagonisten. Seine Einsichten in der Betrachtung dieses großen Künstlers beanspruchen eine Allgemeingültigkeit, die uns auch Hinweise auf die Kunst Dietmar Brixys geben kann. Selbstverständlich betrachten wir die Kunst des Mannheimer Künstlers mit anderen Augen als die Werke derjenigen Künstler des ausgehenden 19. bzw. beginnenden 20. Jahrhunderts. Brixy malt in aller Regel auch nicht vor der Natur, obwohl sein ihn umgebender phänomenaler Garten ihm genug Einblicke geben mag. Wir sprechen hier von einer Ateliermalerei mit Bezug auf Phänomene, die einen Naturbezug haben. Es ist, ganz im Sinne des oben zitierten großen Meisters, eine Annäherung im Sinne einer parallelen Harmonie zur Natur.

Und diese äußert sich nicht in einer geometrisch angelegten Bildstrategie mit Kugel und Zylinder (Cézanne), sondern in einer landschaftlichen Expression, die synästhetische Anklänge hat. Diese Motivwelt mit ihrer lianenartigen Umfassung, mit Assoziationen zu Bergkämmen, Flüssen, Seen, zu Horizont und Himmel, äußert sich in mehrstufiger Koloristik. Brixy schiebt und verschiebt in unterschiedlicher perspektivischer Setzung landschaftliche Blöcke. Seine Technik, Ölfarbe mit Rakel, Spachtel, Kämmen, bisweilen auch mit dem Pinsel und den Fingern zu ziehen, um so die erwünschten Strukturen zu schaffen, ist meisterlich ausgeprägt. Farbe in ihrer Anwendung wird nun definitiv nicht mehr als Matrix für ein Bildgeschehen eingesetzt, wie dies noch bei den früheren Arbeiten der Fall war. Farbe wird in ihrer energetischen und konkret materiellen Qualität betont. Der pastose Auftrag wird diesem Anspruch in idealer Weise gerecht. Auch wenn bei gewissen malerischen Operationen Farbflächen abgekratzt oder eliminiert werden, bleibt das Materielle ansichtig. Farbe ist nun das beherrschende Medium.

So entstehen im Medium der Farbe in kleinen, aber vor allem in großen Formaten Werke mit spezifischen innerbildlichen Ansichten. Gesten bestimmen viele Werke. Sicherlich ist die große, mit den Fingern vornehmlich im oberen Bildbereich gesetzte, vollendende abschließende Geste, die sich in aller Regel über das ganze Bildgeviert ausbreitet, eine Hommage an das Motiv selbst. Der Taktstock bewegt sich hier zum letzten Mal im Sinne einer Beendigung des malerisch-symphonischen Geschehens.

Surprise, 2016
140 × 180 cm

Schauplatz Venedig: Unter dem von Marco Polo inspirierten Titel *The Description of the World* stellt Dietmar Brixy insgesamt 38 Werke aus den Jahren

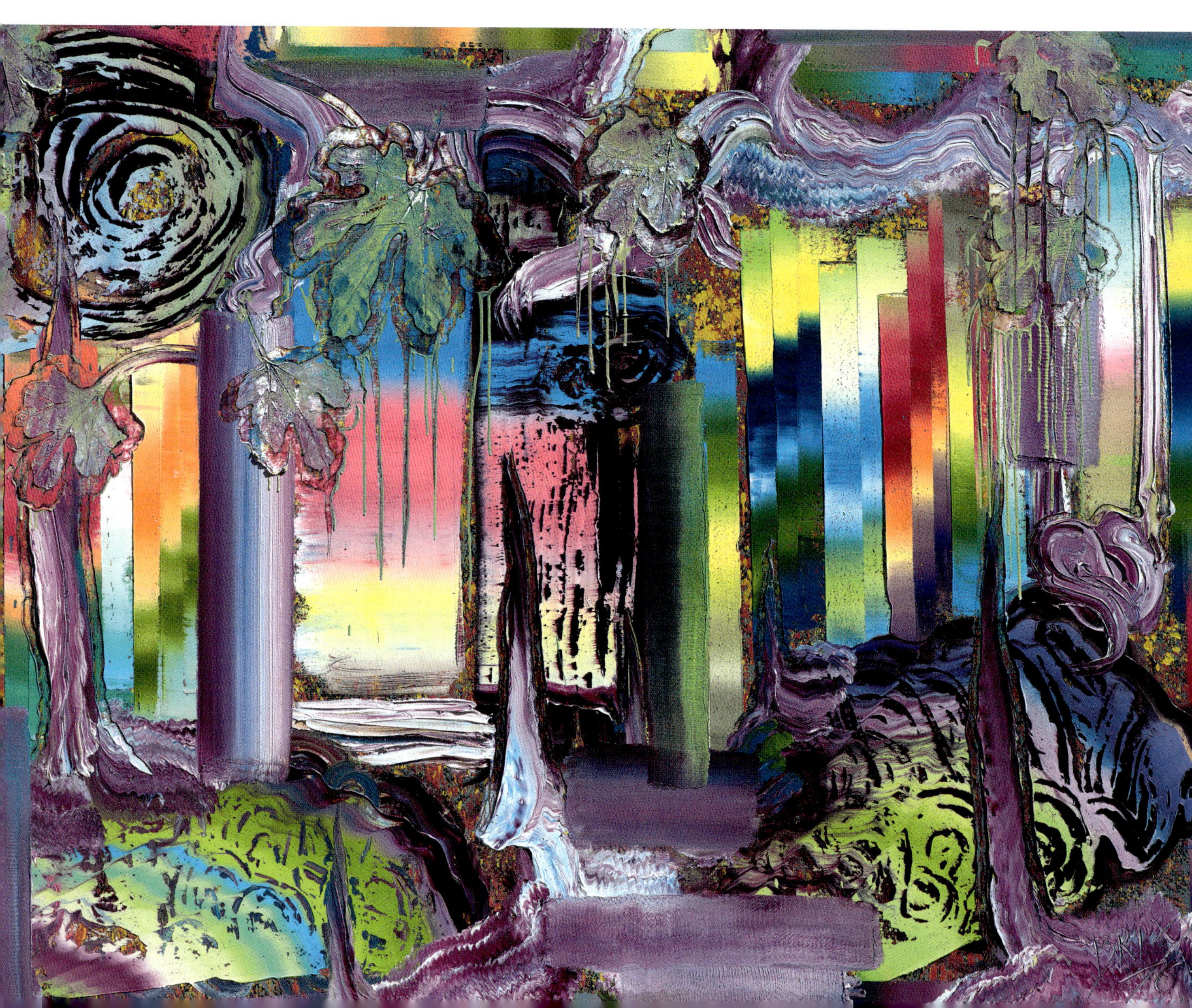

2013 bis 2024 in der Biblioteca Nazionale Marciana aus. Diese 1468 gegründete, ca. eine Million Objekte beherbergende Bibliothek ist eine der wichtigsten und größten Wissensinstitute Italiens mit bedeutenden Sammlungen griechischer, lateinischer und orientalischer Manuskripte. Der heutige Bibliotheksbau wurde 1537 in Auftrag gegeben und 1591 vollendet. Er steht am Ort der größten Repräsentanz der damaligen Republik Venedig – am Markusplatz. Der bedeutende Architekt Andrea Palladio definierte das Gebäude als „das vielleicht kostbarste und prunkvollste Gebäude, das seit der Antike entstanden ist".[7] Hierzu zählen Gemälde im Bereich des Treppenhauses und der ehemaligen Lesesäle von den besten Künstlern Italiens: Veronese, Tizian und Tintoretto.

Der vielgereiste, weltberühmte Venezianer Marco Polo ist für Dietmar Brixy in vielerlei Hinsicht ein bedeutendes Vorbild. Brixys Expeditionen führten ihn auch in solch ferne, bisweilen exotische Welten wie Malaysia, Mexiko, Indien, Bali, Thailand und die Seychellen. Daher war er sich sehr bewusst, an welch geschichtsträchtigem Ort seine Werke in Venedig ausgestellt werden. So hat er für das Vestibül eine für sein Œuvre gänzlich neue, raumgreifende Arbeit entwickelt, ein Oktogon mit einer Höhe von ca. drei Metern. Acht Bildtafeln nehmen Bezug auf die Deckendekoration darüber: Tizians achteckiges Deckengemälde auf Leinwand: *La Sapienza – Weisheit* (177 × 177 cm, Abb. S. 38), eine auf Wolken sitzende elegante Frauenfigur im roten Gewand, als Allegorie der Weisheit gedeutet, mit einem weißlichen Schriftband in ihrer linken Hand. Die rechte Hand hält einen Spiegel, den ein Cupido stützt. Mit dieser außerordentlichen achteckigen Komposition überstrahlt Tizian alle anderen Gemälde im Treppenhaus sowie dem großen Lesesaal: Ansporn genug für einen Maler der Moderne, sich mit diesem bedeutenden Werk auseinanderzusetzen. Weisheit ist jenseits aller Kulturen und Epochen eine Bestandsaufnahme für unsere Daseinsorientierung und insofern für jeden Maler eine Herausforderung, ganz gleich welche bildlichen Ereignisse das Ergebnis sein werden.

In Dietmar Brixys Oktogon aus dem Jahr 2024 werden wir durch eine umfangreiche Landschaftserzählung geleitet, die seine bisherigen Bilder insofern übertrifft, als wir das achteckige Werk zu umschreiten haben, um zu einer optischen Synthese zu gelangen. Einmal erfolgt, kann die Sehaufgabe wieder von Neuem beginnen, immer im Dialog mit der über ihr schwebenden Weisheit. Nähert man sich diesem optisch herausfordernden Oktogon, so erfährt man schon mit dem ersten Blick, dass Dietmar Brixy uns in landschaftliche Traumwelten mitnimmt. Den uns begegnenden Bildkosmos in seiner Simultanität können wir uns nur durch kleine optische Schritte erarbeiten, von unten nach oben, von links nach rechts und vice versa. An Bildkanten sehen wir Verbindungen zu den nächsten Tafeln links und rechts. Die großen gestischen Schwingungen begegnen uns wieder in den Bildabschlüssen des oberen Fünftels: Unter ihnen geschichtete Welten, die sowohl nahegelegene als auch ferne Welten zeigen. Berge, Bäume, Pflanzen im Modus einer phantasievollen Koloristik sind hier die Bildhelden. Es ist vor allem auch das Licht, das uns in bisweilen abenteuerlichen Farbzusammenhängen begegnet.

Dieses Oktogon strahlt in alle Richtungen des Vestibüls und nimmt daher Bezug zum historischen Raum. Diese Raumeinnahme, dieser Prolog wird im großen Lesesaal weitergeführt mit den Serien *Happy*, *Reflect* und *Journey*. Hinzu kommt an der Stirnwand dieses machtvollen Raums eine Installation mit neun *Bamboo Bubbles*, jenen rundformatigen Gemälden, die gerade in der Renaissance durch Künstler wie Michelangelo neue Ausdrucksformen erhielten. Der Kreis ist immer mit der Idee von Perfektion verbunden. Insofern haben die *Bamboo Bubbles* eine besondere Bedeutung im Werk des Künstlers und schaffen hier den Bezug zu den in der Biblioteca Marciana vorzufindenden Tondi der italienischen Künstler. Zugleich sind die modernen Tondi eine Referenz an die kunstvoll runden Weltkarten in der Sammlung der Bibliothek. Und vereinzelt nehmen diese an der Stirnwand platzierten Werke auch in der italienischen Renaissance und im Frühbarock beliebte Farben auf, vom Veroneser Grün bis zum Tizianrot. Selbstverständlich überbietet der moderne Maler diese Palette mit seinen spezifischen Farben wie Pink, Türkisgrün oder Kobaltblau. Ein spannender venezianischer Dialog, der in den zukünftigen Werken Dietmar Brixys seinen Niederschlag finden wird.

[1] Rainer Maria Rilke äußerte sich so in seiner Einleitung zu: Auguste Rodin. Erster Teil, zit. nach: Rilke. Werke, Bd. 3, 4. Aufl. Frankfurt am Main 1986, S. 351.

[2] Maris Denis, Définition du néo-traditionnisme, in: Art et Critique, 23. August 1890, S. 540, übers. nach: Alessandra Tiddia, Auf den Spuren von Maurice Denis. Symbolismus an den Grenzen des Habsburger Reichs, Mailand 2007, S. 35.

[3] Vincent van Gogh an Theo van Gogh, 4. Mai 1888, zit. nach Fritz Erpel (Hg.), Vincent van Gogh. Sämtliche Briefe, Bd. 4, Berlin 1965, S. 40.

[4] Paul Klee, Nr. 9260, in: Tagebücher von Paul Klee. 1898–1918, hg. von Felix Klee, Köln 1995, S. 350.

[5] Friedrich Nietzsche, Also sprach Zarathustra, in: Werke in vier Bänden, hg. von G. Stenzel, Bd. 1, Salzburg 1983, S. 297.

[6] Peter Handke, Die Lehre der Sainte Victoire, Frankfurt am Main 1984, S. 61f.

[7] Zit. nach: Filippo Pedrocco, Tizian, München 2000, S. 267.

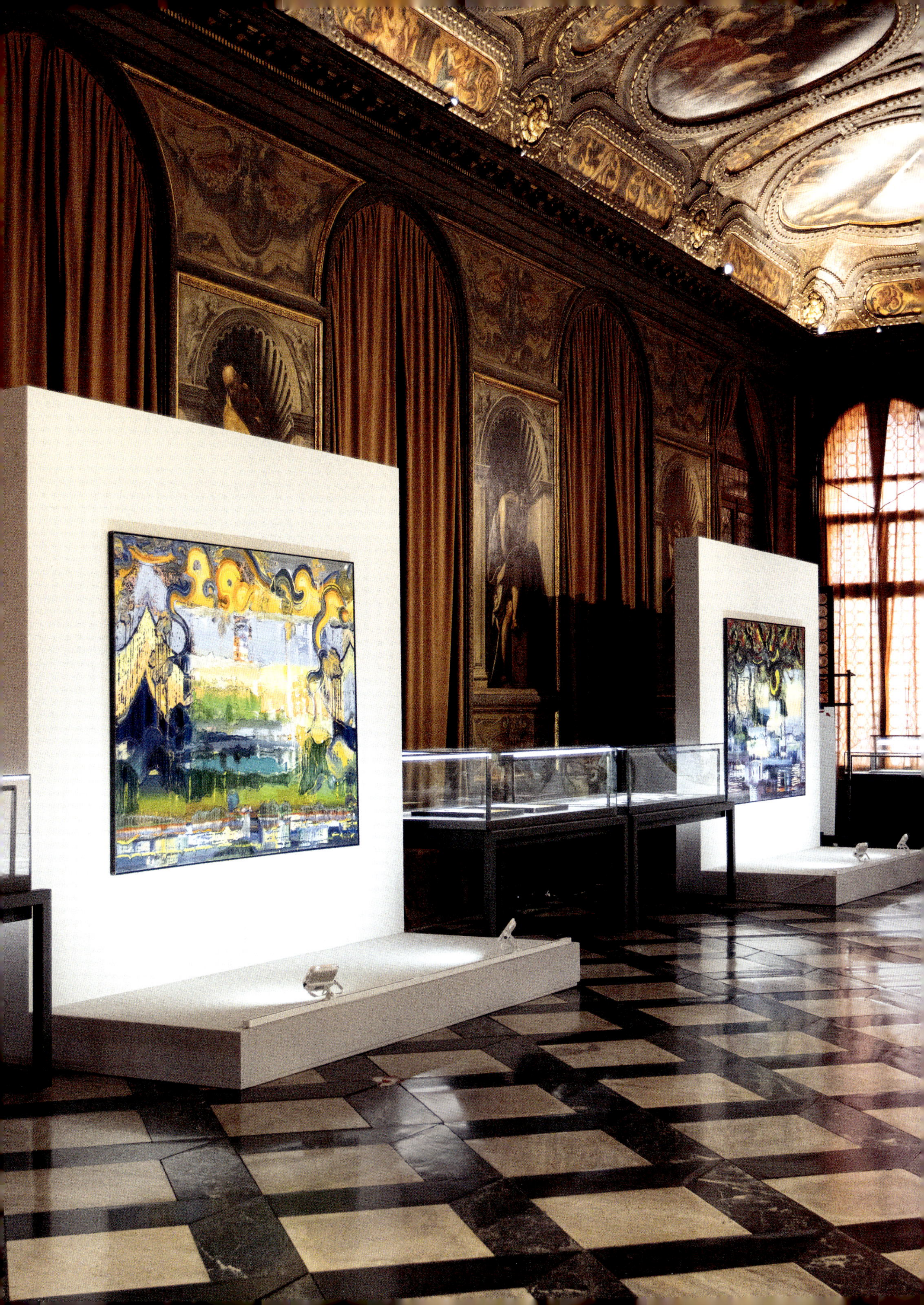

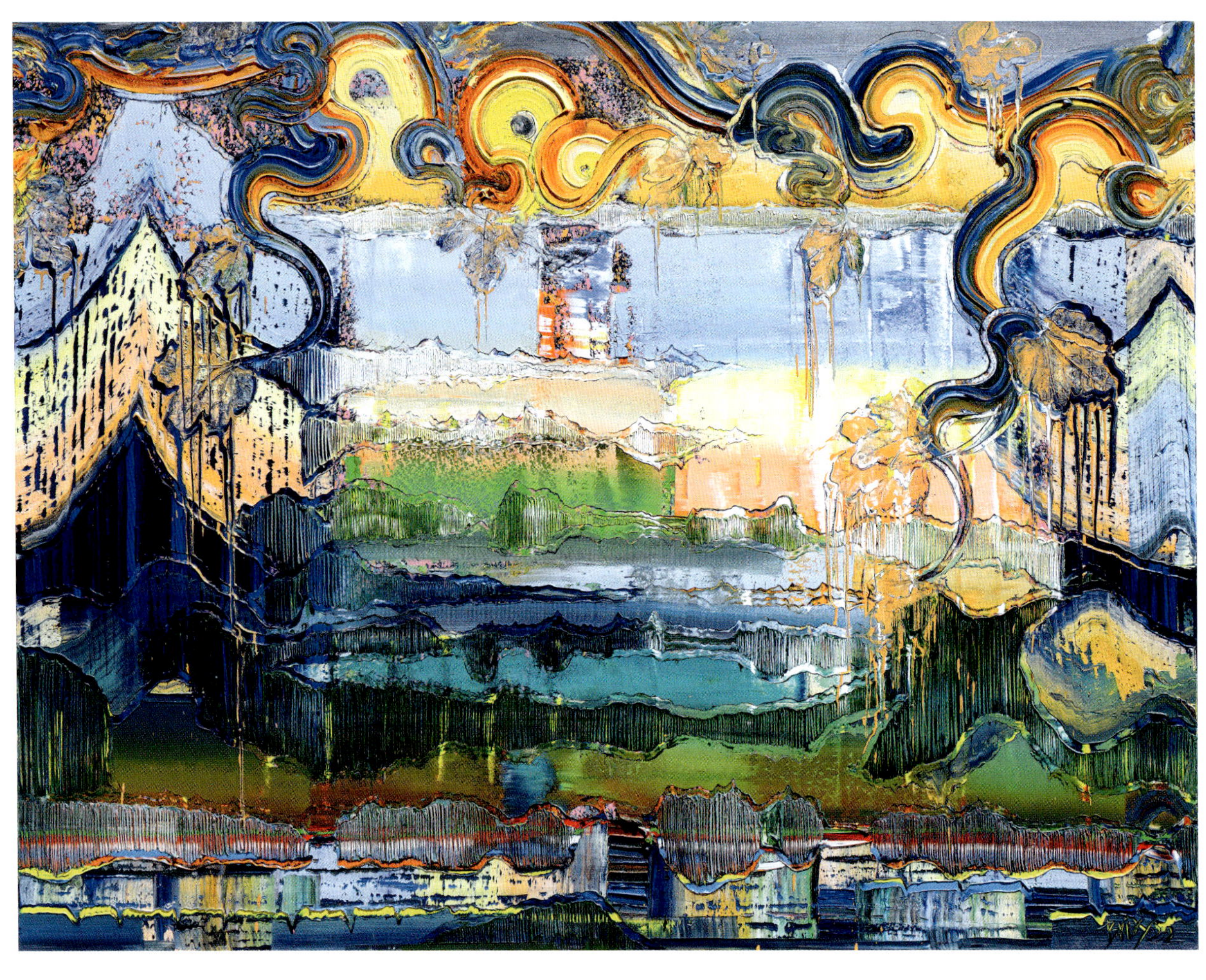

Journey, 2022
160 × 210 cm
S. / pp. 32/33: Detail

DIETMAR BRIXY CONNECTED

Dr. Tayfun Belgin

"The work that is to be spoken of in these pages developed through long years. It has grown like a forest and has not lost one hour."[1]

And so, too, the art of Dietmar Brixy has for long years forged ahead, in a sensitive aesthetic that, while not exactly free of inner tension, still emerges into a wondrous habitat all of its own. The works coalesce into an artistic world at once inwardly self-referential and outwardly held in the close embrace of nature and its coloristic abundance: trees, plants, shrubs, and all manner of flowers; a stock of imagery symbolic of the city dweller's passion for nature.

With his acquisition of a former pumping station in Mannheim-Neckarau, the painter, draughtsman, and sculptor Dietmar Brixy has created a paradise of a studio, where he frequently receives interested guests. There we encounter a lover of nature who approaches the object of his admiration first and foremost in his opulent paintings, only to quietly bid farewell again – until the next canvas, that is. But are these paintings really depictions of Nature with a capital N? Are we not succumbing to a wonderful illusion when we attempt to influence our eyes, our minds, with such a rational assertion? Let us offer an initial answer to this question via the Symbolist Maurice Denis, painter, theorist, and co-founder of the Nabis, who reminded his readers in the magazine *Art et Critique* in 1890:

"We should remember that a picture – before being a war horse, a nude woman, or telling some other story – is essentially a flat surface covered with colors arranged in a particular pattern."[2]

A momentous sentence for modernism – with eternal validity, so to say. It is not yet an appeal for pure abstraction in painting – we hadn't quite reached that point yet – but rather an appeal to reflect on what constituted a picture (at that time), a painting that is aware of its stylistic means and does not merely represent the extra-pictorial. Denis's insight is essential for modern painting: rather than declaring the death of painting, he showed that its role was to change. Painters were well aware that, as a visual record of moments in time, photography was already hot on their heels. Vincent van Gogh's famous statement, "But the painter of the future is a colorist,"[3] obviously also takes on a deeper meaning in this context. Although van Gogh was speaking for himself and his own art, his insight, too, is fundamental. Nor did it end there: Paul Klee was the first in the twentieth century

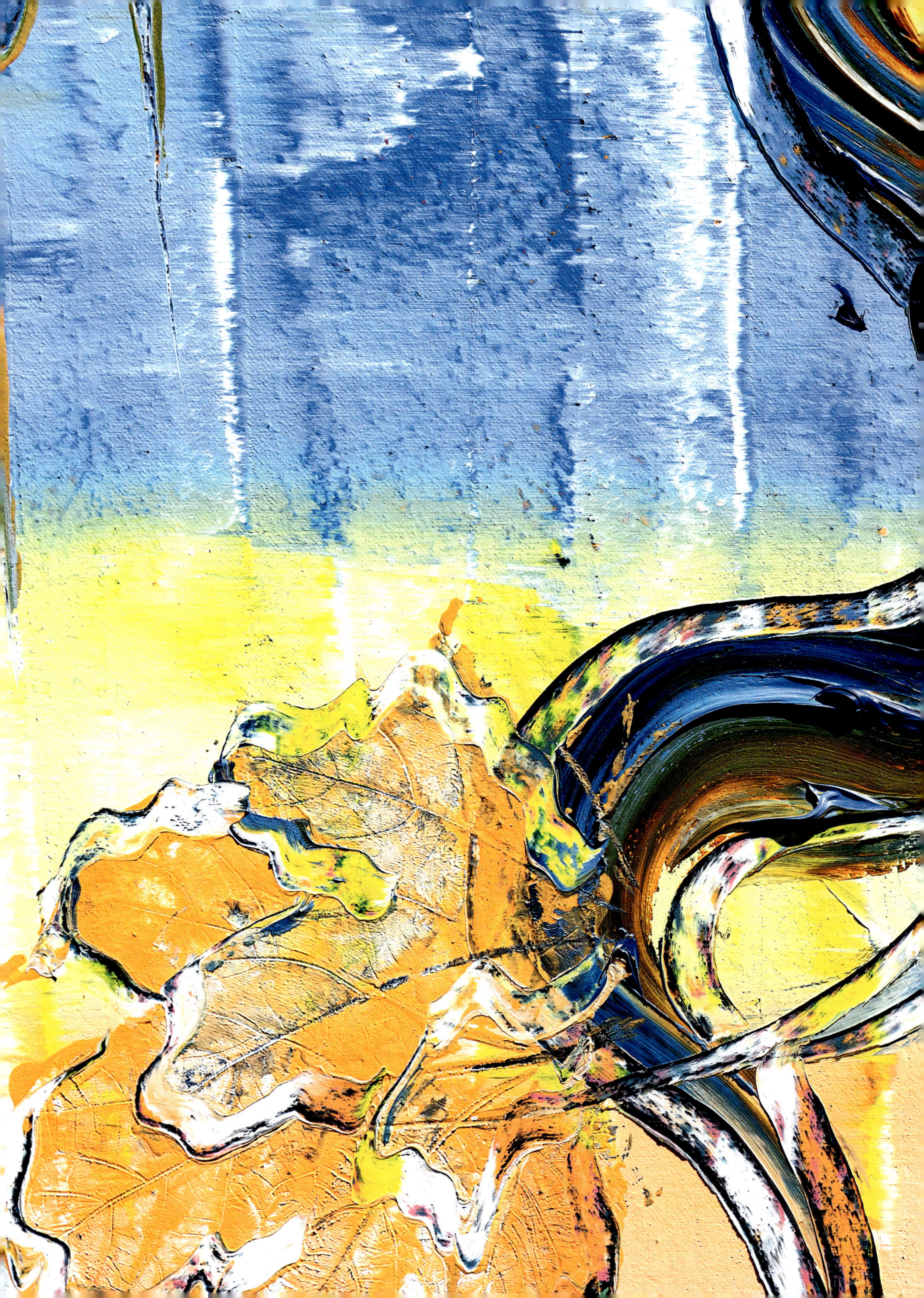

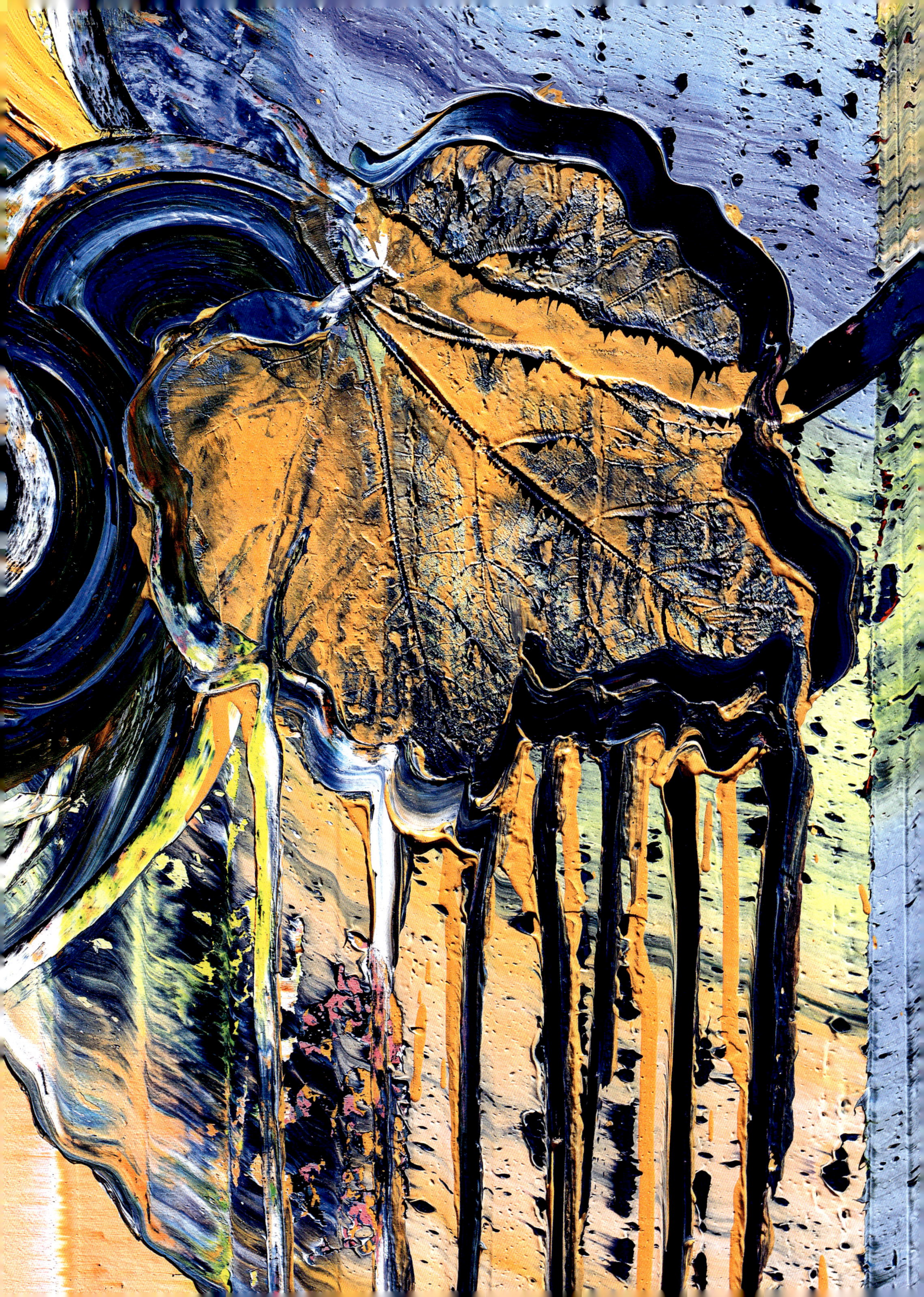

to confirm the importance of color, in a diary entry from Kairouan during his trip to Tunis on April 16, 1914: "Color possesses me. I don't have to pursue it. It will possess me always, I know it. That is the meaning of this happy hour: Color and I are one. I am a painter."[4]

Completed before his move to the now-renowned former pumping station in 2003, Brixy's early paintings were characterized by an entirely different temperament than the boldly colorful works of today. For him, color was undoubtedly the defining means of artistic expression. His established technique of applying and later removing layers of paint developed impressively over the years and still determines the current polyvalent colorism that so electrifies collectors. In conversation, however, Brixy points out that he had already mastered this technique as a child and relishes bringing forth small-format juvenilia to prove his point (Untitled, 1968, wax crayon on paper, 28 × 21 cm, p. 20)

In the works of the 1990s, we generally see a multi-layered dialog of colors and forms. Here, color almost always serves as a matrix for porous forms, thrown down onto the canvas as in action painting, with outlines that suggest human figures, but also barely discernable natural shapes such as snail shells, plants, and trees (Untitled, 1991, oil on canvas, 240 × 180 cm, p. 24). Much of it appears as insubstantial as breath, about to dissolve or on the cusp of transformation into abstract signs. With a great deal of imagination, some of these largely androgynous forms could also be interpreted as warriors with shields afloat in the pictorial space. Sometimes they gather around a ladder, or rush across the canvas, or even drift down into the pictorial space from above.

In these energetic paintings, we see the essence of Dietmar Brixy's visual language begin to emerge. As a painter, his preferred strategy is suggestion, placing in the world forms and figures whose clarity nevertheless remains a secret. In the beginning, these works were still given titles like *Swimmer*, *Sunken*, *Jungle Creatures*, or *Found*, which still refer to some external reality, no matter how abstractly it may be staged. In this world of appearing and disappearing forms, the viewers must create the image for themselves. Despite the works' painterly refinement, clarity is strategically denied. No horizon can be perceived. The relationship between horizontality and verticality, our existential reference to reality, is abandoned in favor of a creative, yet disorderly pictorial world.

Colors and forms cram these pictorial spaces to bursting point. These works are processes, seeming to follow one another in a logic determined by their content. Brixy hints at a pictorial event, but declines to position himself clearly. The vibrant pictorial space seems to be subordinated to a state of chaos – although this term should not be understood in its Ancient Greek sense, as the lightless maw of the underworld, but rather in a modern sense. Here we see imagery and envisioned spaces imbued with potential energies, something like harbingers of a universal order. Brixy's paintings play through the oppositions of order and chaos, both of which are evident and characterize his pictorial strategy in this period.

To put it positively, let us turn to Nietzsche, who has his Zarathustra proclaim to the people: “I tell you: one must still have chaos in one, to give birth to a dancing star.”[5]

Scene change: the curtain rises. After 20 years, Dietmar Brixy's choice of imagery has transformed to such an extent that we are momentarily left quite speechless. We could not have foreseen the radicalness of the pictorial spaces now confronting us. Brixy opens up a pictorial event that we perceive from a kind of stage; he takes us by the hand and leads us into a pictorial event blown up to the scale of a panorama. We look from left to right, from top to bottom, stopping briefly to pause at one point in the middle. Faced with this powerful rhythm of color, this colorism taken from nature and its infinite phenomena, all we can do is look on in wonder.

“Once, when Cézanne was asked to explain what he meant by a motif, he slowly joined the outspread fingers of his two hands together, folded and interlocked them. Reading about this, I remembered that in looking at this picture I had seen the pines and rocks as intertwined letters, their meaning as clear as it was indefinable. In one of Cézanne's letters I read that he did not paint ‘from nature’ – that his pictures were ‘constructions and harmonies parallel to nature’.”[6]

In the quote above, Peter Handke interprets Cézanne's works with linguistic sensitivity. But his insights into this great artist have a general validity that can also give us clues to Brixy's art. Naturally, we look at the art of a contemporary painter from Mannheim with different eyes than we do the works of those artists of the late nineteenth and early twentieth centuries. As a rule, Brixy does not paint ‘from nature,’ either, although the extraordinary garden that surrounds his studio may provide insight enough. Yet we are speaking here of studio painting that deals with phenomena which have a direct connection to the natural world. Brixy's approach, in the spirit of Cézanne referenced above, is one of harmonies parallel to the natural world.

His approach, however, is not expressed through a geometric strategy involving cones, spheres, and cylinders (as with Cézanne), but rather as a kind of landscape with synesthetic resonance. This world of motifs, with its liana-like embrace, its evocations of mountains, rivers, lakes, horizons, and skies, is expressed in multiple layers of coloration. In different perspectival settings, Brixy transports and transposes blocks of landscape. His technique of creating the desired textures by applying oil paint with squeegees, palette knives, combs, and sometimes also brushes as well as his fingers is nothing short of masterful.

The application of color certainly no longer serves as a matrix for a pictorial event, as it did in the earlier works. Color itself is now emphasized in its energetic and concrete material quality. The impasto application is ideally suited to this requirement; even if areas of color are scraped off or jettisoned in certain painterly operations, the material remains visible. Color itself is now the dominant medium.

This medium of color gives rise to small- and, above all, large-format works with specific, inward pictorial views. Many of them are shaped by gestures. Without doubt, the large, final gesture of completion made with the fingers, primarily in the upper part of the picture, though usually extending over the entire space, is a homage to the motif itself. The conductor's baton beats time here for one last moment to conclude the symphonic action in paint.

Scene: Venice
Under the title *The Description of the World*, inspired by none other than Marco Polo himself, Dietmar Brixy is exhibiting a total of thirty-eight works from the years 2013 to 2024 in the Biblioteca Nazionale Marciana. Founded in 1468 and housing approximately one million items, this library is one of the largest and most important scholarly institutes in Italy, with significant collections of Greek, Latin, and Byzantine manuscripts. The current building, commissioned in 1537 and completed in 1591, stands on Saint Mark's Square, opposite the seat of government of the former Republic of Venice. The famous Renaissance architect Andrea Palladio defined the building as "perhaps the richest and most ornate building that has been built since antiquity."[7] The library's collection includes paintings by Venice's most renowned artists – such as Veronese, Titian, and Tintoretto – displayed in the stairwell and former reading rooms.

In many respects, the famous Venetian traveler Marco Polo is an important role model for Brixy. The painter's expeditions have also taken him to such distant, exotic places as Malaysia, Mexico, India, Bali, Thailand, and the Seychelles. He was therefore very aware of the historic importance of his exhibition site in Venice and has created for it a completely new, expansive work to be displayed in the vestibule, an octagon approximately three meters wide (*Endless Journey*, 2024, octagon, 8 boards, each 300 × 70 cm, p. 14). Its eight panels refer to the ceiling decoration above it: Titian's octagonal canvas *La Sapienza* (177 × 177 cm, fig. p. 38), wich depicts an elegant, red-robed female figure, interpreted as an allegory of wisdom, seated on a cushion of billowing clouds. A whitish scroll is draped over her left hand, while her right holds a mirror supported by a Cupid. Titian's extraordinary octagonal composition outshines all other paintings in the stairwell and spacious reading room – incentive enough for a modern painter to engage with this important work. Across all cultures and epochs, wisdom is a measure of our grip on reality and therefore an abiding challenge to every painter, regardless of what pictorial events may result.

In Brixy's octagon from 2024, we are guided through an extensive landscape narrative that surpasses his previous efforts insofar as we must circumambulate the entire work in order to arrive at an optical synthesis.

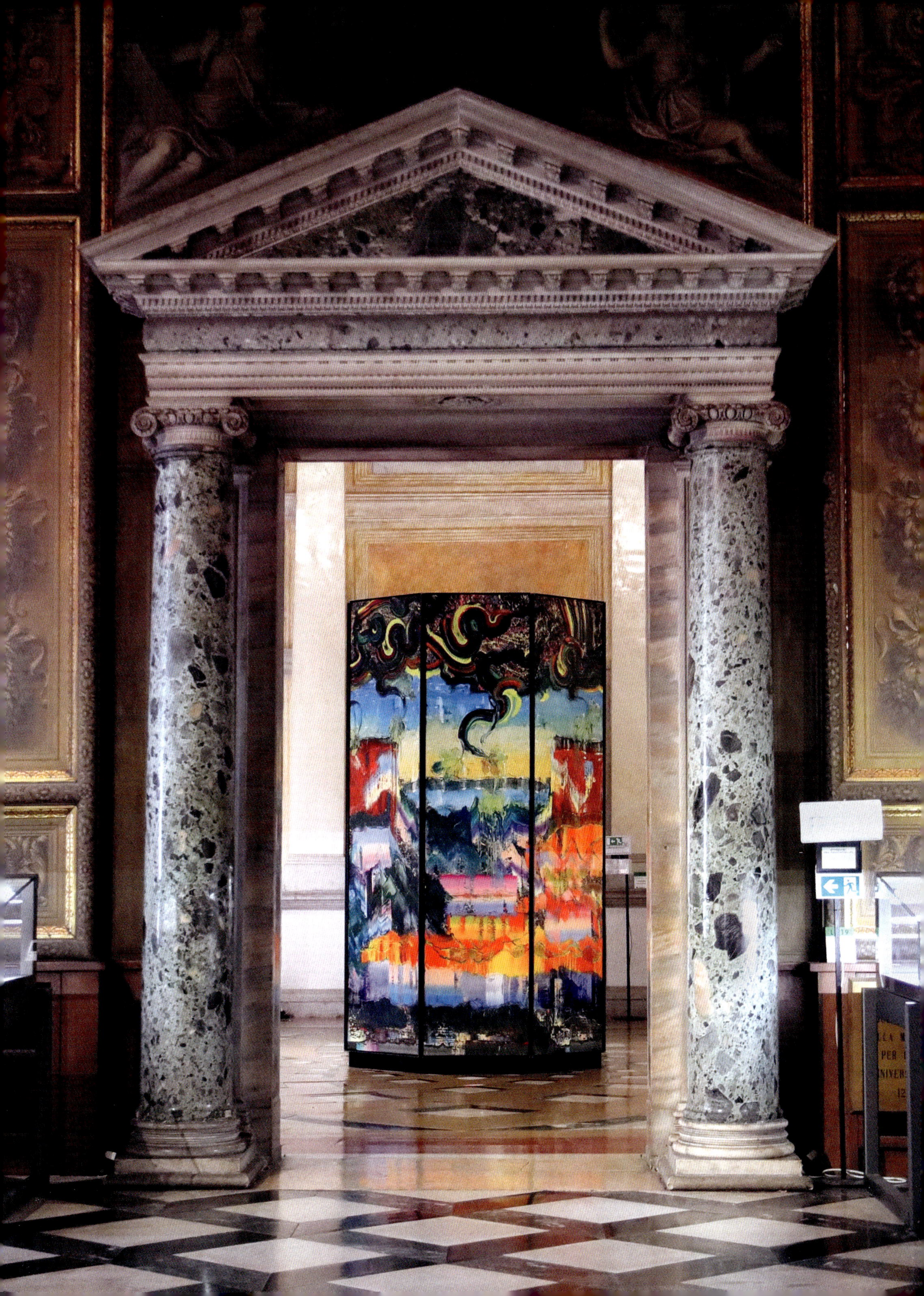

Once this has been achieved, the work of seeing can begin anew, always in dialog with the *Wisdom* poised above it. As we approach this visually challenging octagon, we realize at first glance that Brixy is taking us into a dreamworld of landscape. We can only work out the simultaneity of the pictorial cosmos we encounter by taking small optical steps, from bottom to top, from left to right and vice versa. At the edges of the picture we see connections to the adjacent panels on the left and right. We encounter the large gestural oscillations again at the edge of the upper fifth of the picture. Worlds, both distant and near, are layered among them. Mountains, trees, and plants depicted in a mode of imaginative coloration are the protagonists here. Above all, it is light that we encounter in these at times daring relations of color.

By radiating in all directions of the vestibule, the octagon refers to the historical space. This occupation of space, this prologue, is continued in the next large reading room with the series *Happy*, *Reflect*, and *Journey*. In addition, there is an installation on the front wall of this commanding room with nine *Bamboo Bubbles*, round-format tondi of the genre that was given new forms of expression in the Renaissance by artists such as Michelangelo. The circle has always been associated with the idea of perfection; in this respect, the *Bamboo Bubbles* have a special significance in Brixy's œuvre, creating a link to the Italian tondi found in the Biblioteca Marciana. At the same time, the modern tondi allude to the artfully round maps of the world in the library's collection. Occasionally, some of these works on the front

Tizian, La Sapienza, 1560, 177 × 177 cm

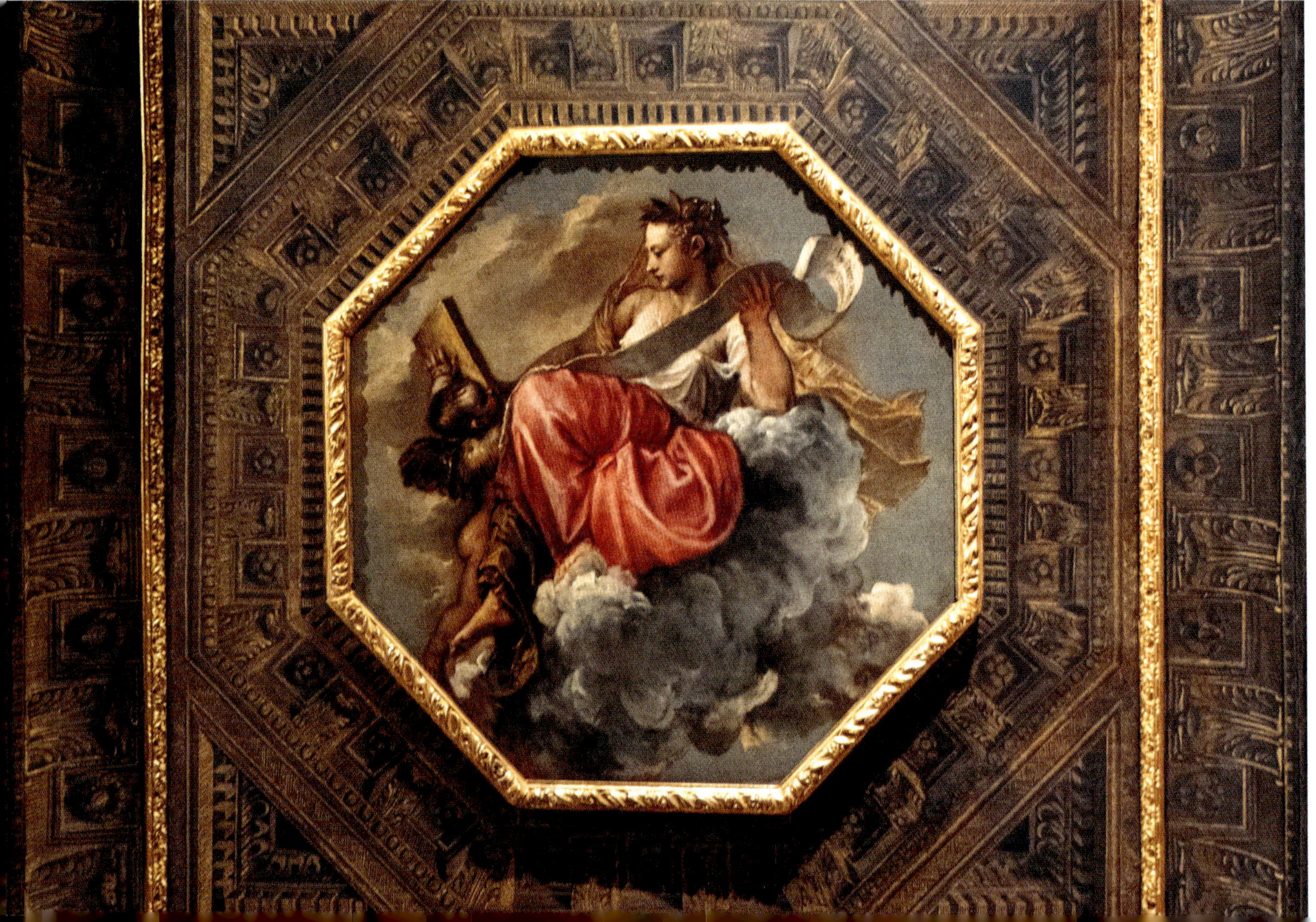

wall also incorporate colors popular during the Italian Renaissance and early Baroque, from Veronese green to Titian red. The modern painter, of course, surpasses this palette by incorporating his own signature colors like pink, turquoise, and cobalt blue. In short, the exhibition represents an exciting Venetian dialog that will no doubt continue to reverberate through Dietmar Brixy's works of the coming years.

---

[1] Rainer Maria Rilke, *Introduction to Auguste Rodin*, trans. Jessie Lemont and Hans Trausil (New York 1919), p. 13.

[2] Maris Denis, "Définition du néo-traditionnisme," in: *Art et Critique*, August 23, 1890, p. 540. Translation by Peter Collier taken from "Maurice Denis (1870–1943), 'Definition of Neo-Traditionalism,'" in: *Art in Theory 1815–1900: An Anthology of Changing Ideas*, ed. Charles Harrison, Paul Wood, and Jason Gaiger (London 1998), p. 862.

[3] Vincent van Gogh to Theo van Gogh, May 4, 1888, The Van Gogh Letters Project, URL: https://vangoghletters.org/vg/letters/let604/letter.html.

[4] Paul Klee, *The Diaries of Paul Klee, 1898–1918*, ed. Felix Klee (Berkeley et al. 1992), no. 9260.

[5] Friedrich Nietzsche, *Thus Spake Zarathustra*, trans. Thomas Common (New York 1917), p. 11.

[6] Peter Handke, *Slow Homecoming*, trans. Ralph Mannheim (New York 1985), p. 178.

[7] Quoted in Filippo Pedrocco, *Tizian* (Munich 2000), p. 267.

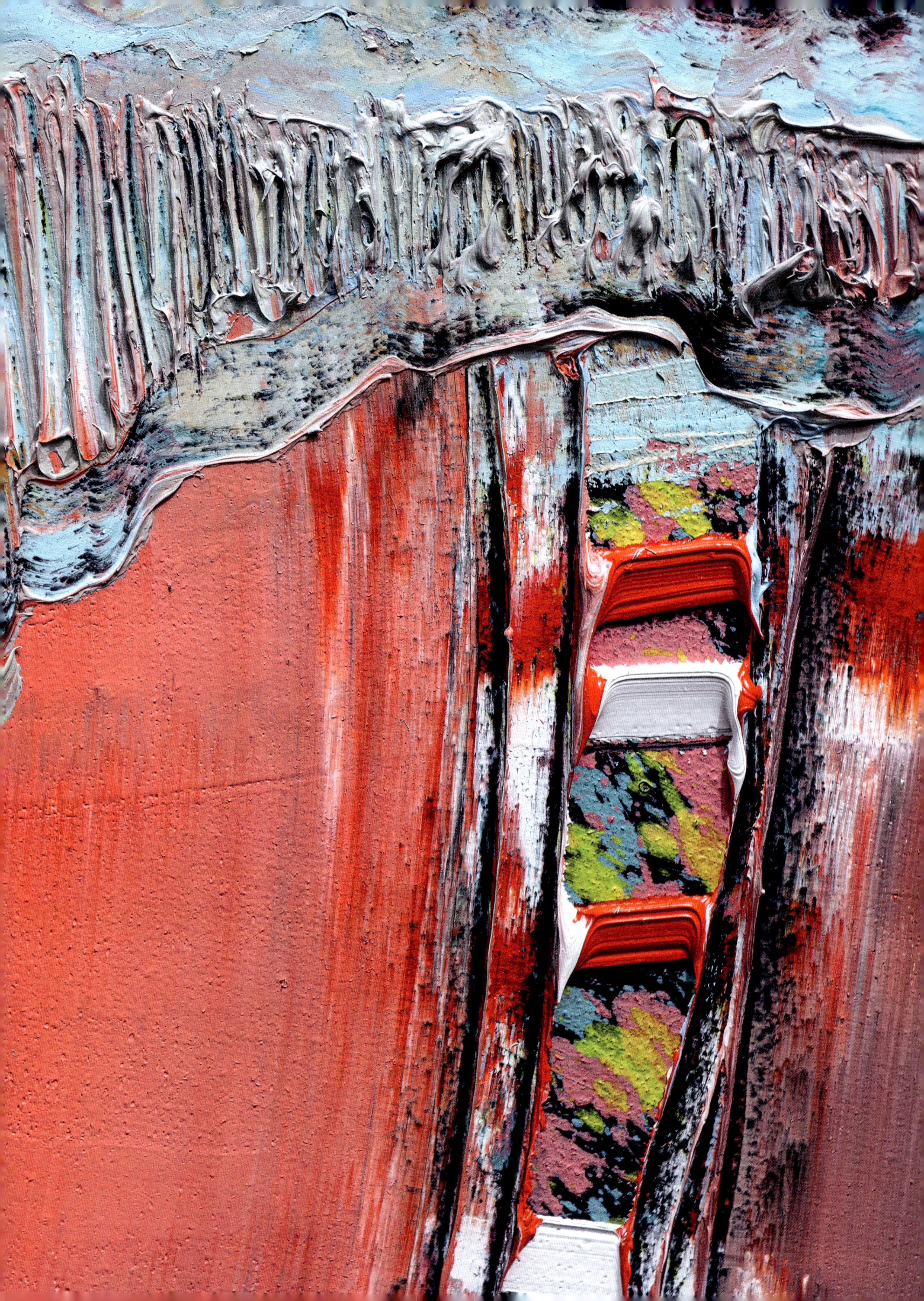

»DAS LEBEN ALS REISE,
ALS WEGSUCHE.«

»LIFE AS A JOURNEY,
AS A SEARCH FOR A PATH.«

Dietmar Brixy

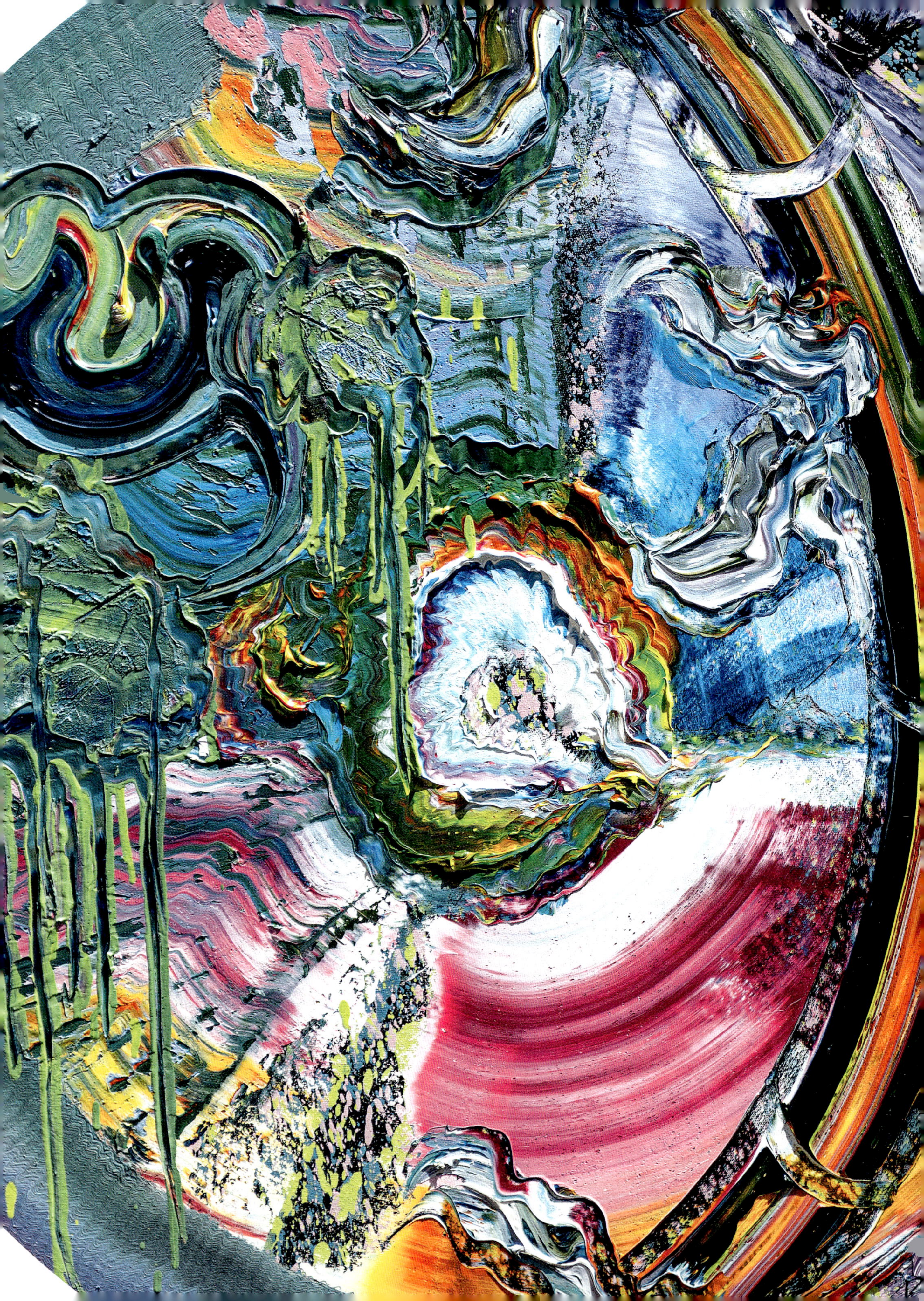

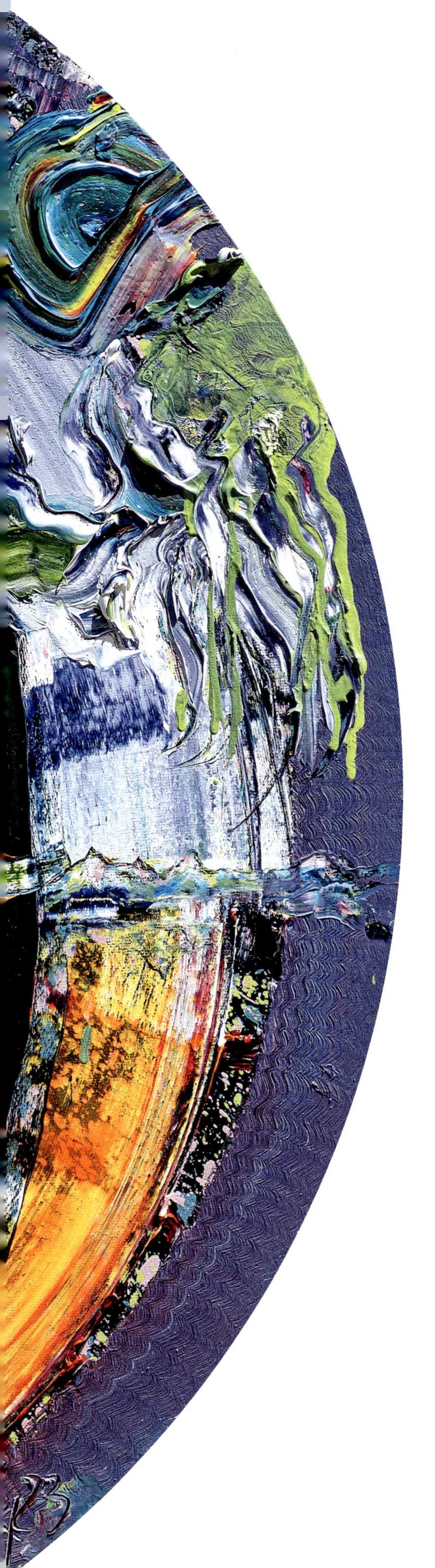

TONDI

ROUND PAINTINGS

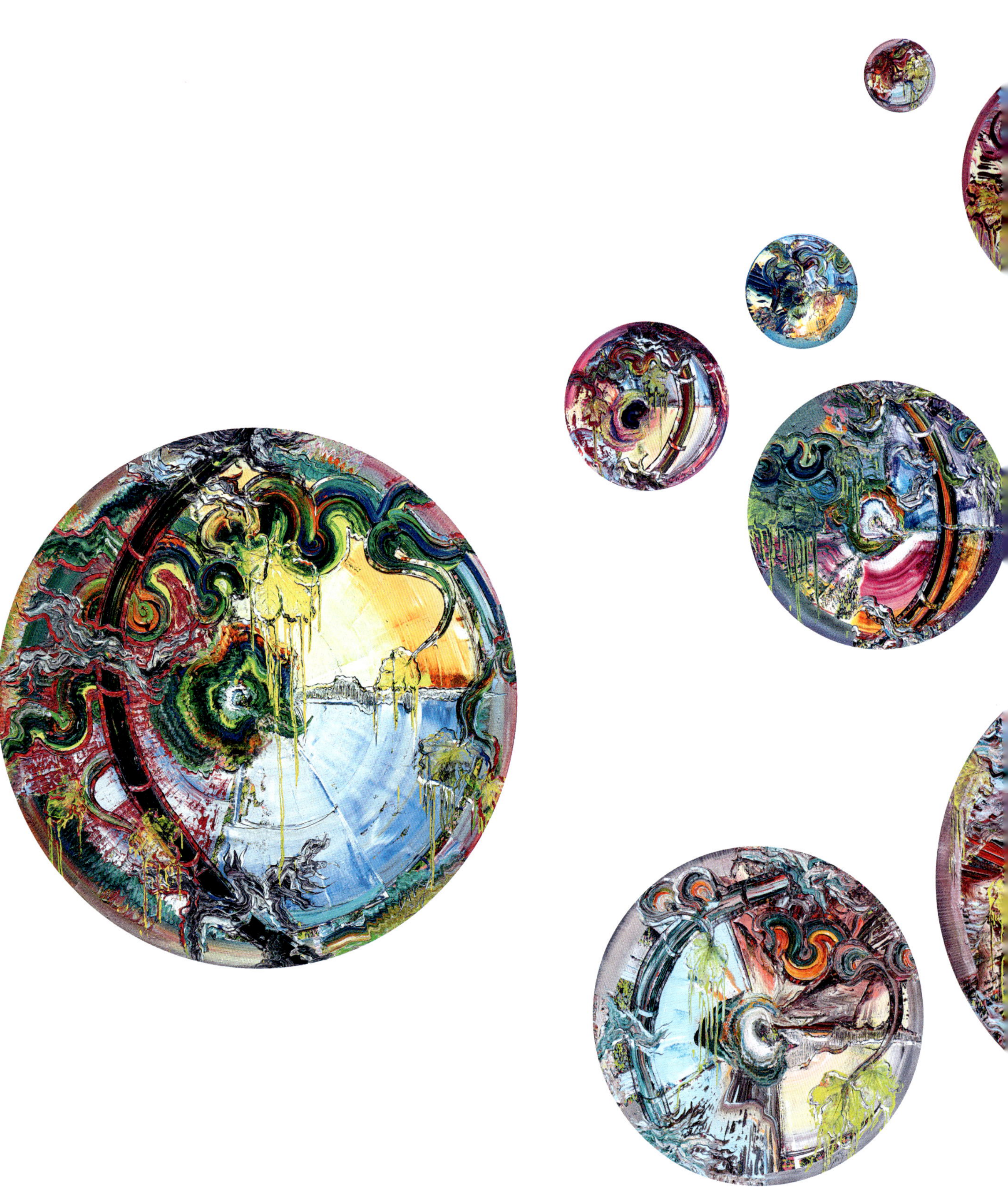

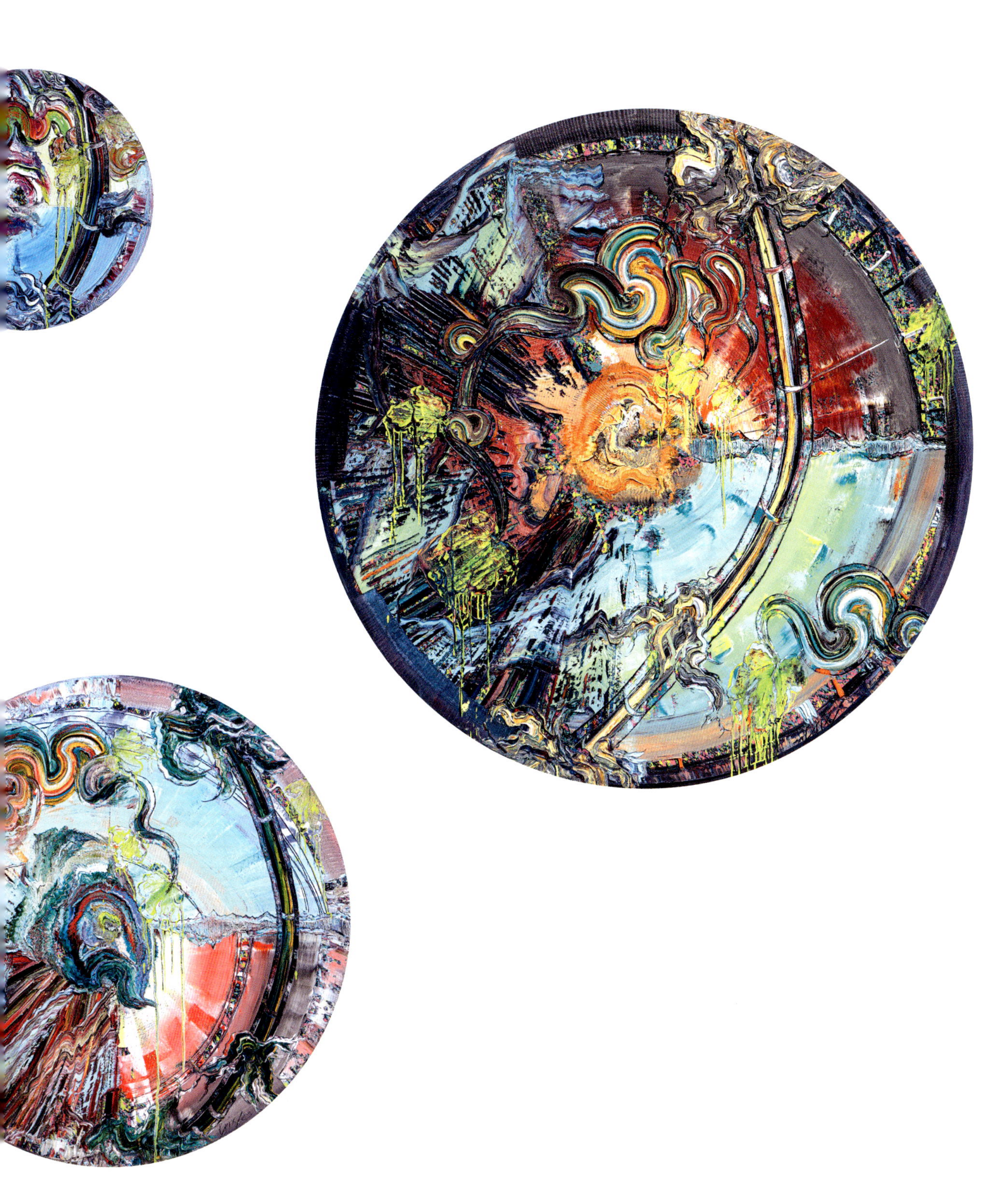

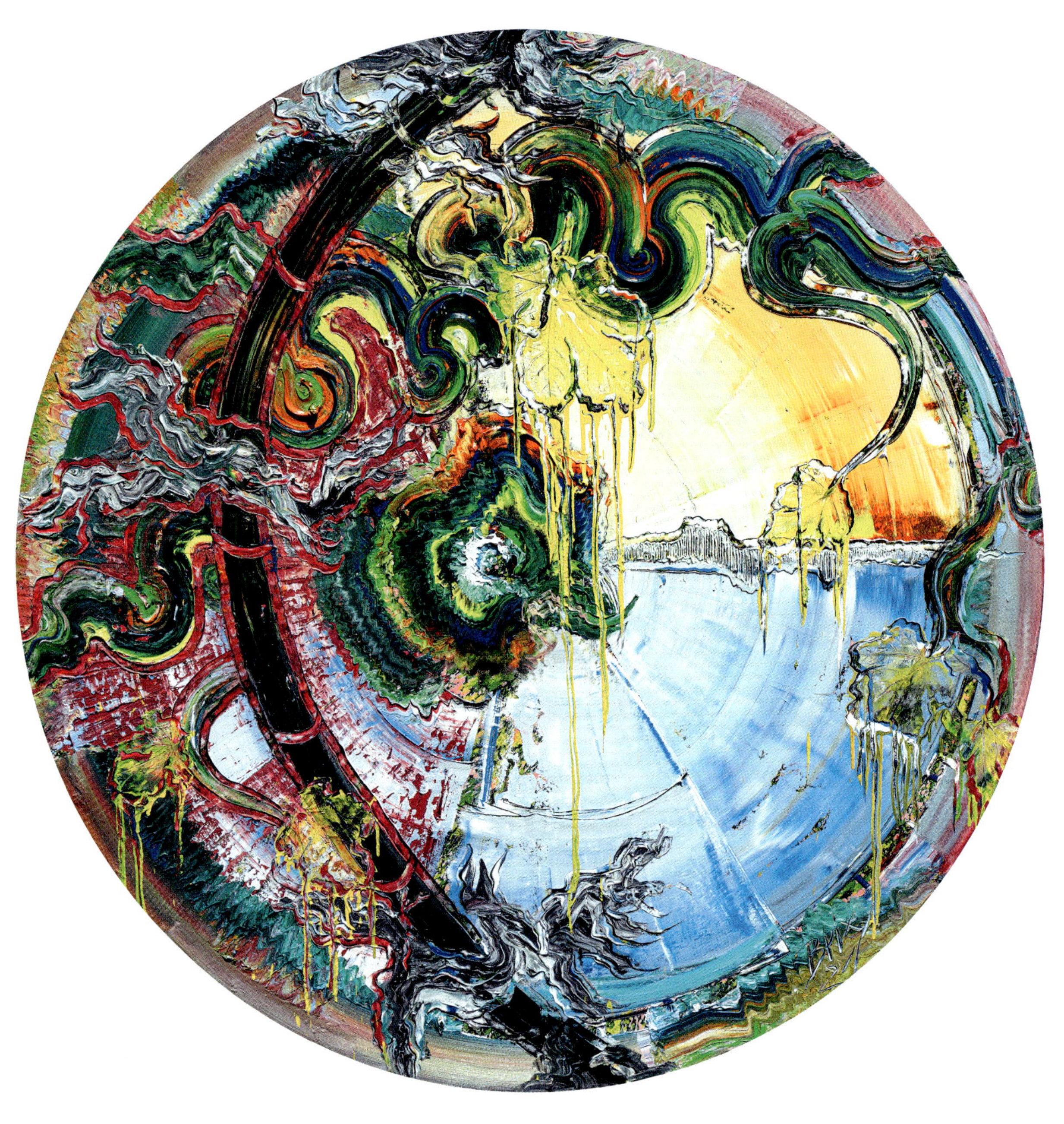

End of Innocence Bamboo Bubble
2021, ø 160 cm

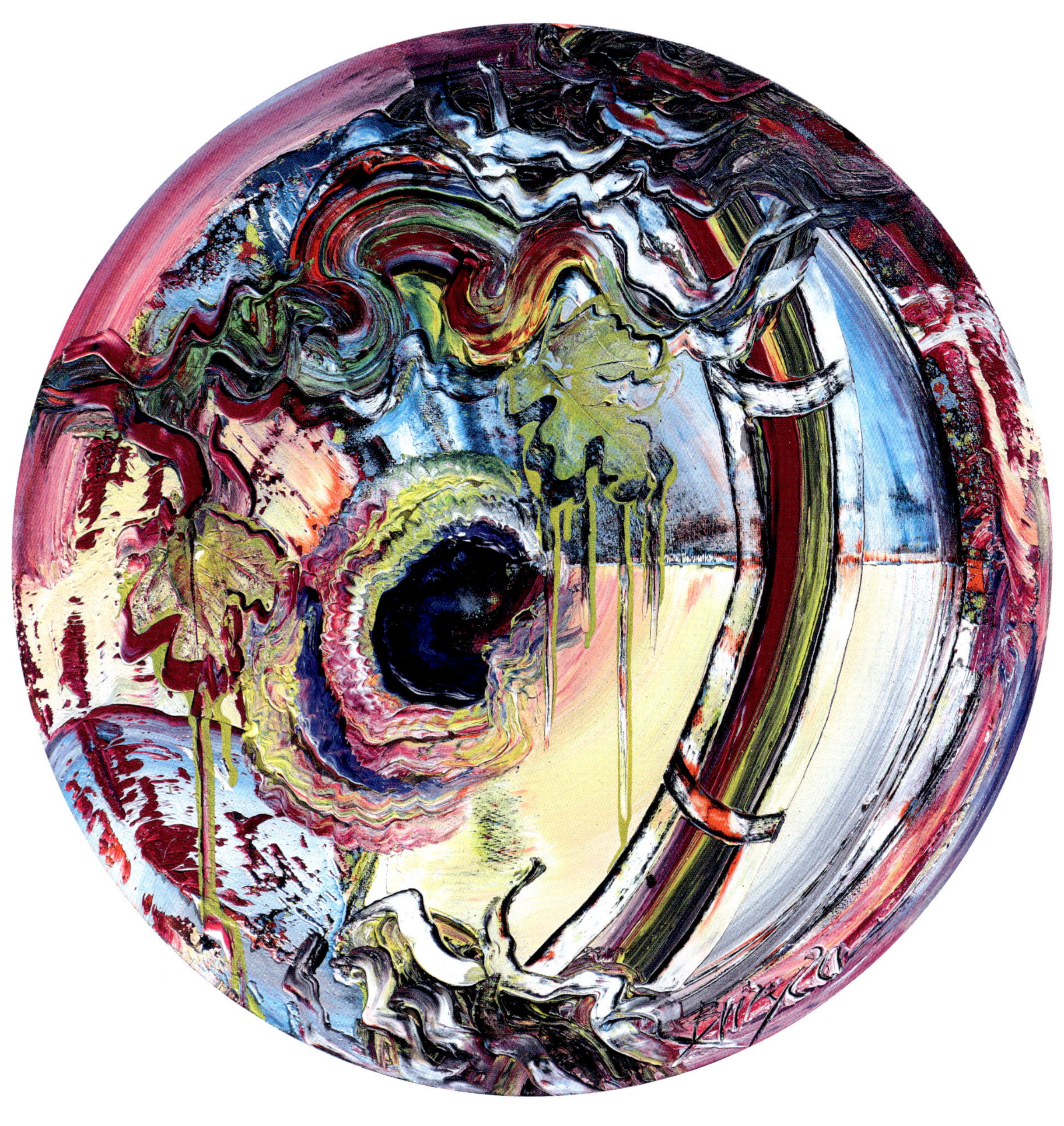

Southern Summer Bamboo Bubble
2020, ø 50 cm

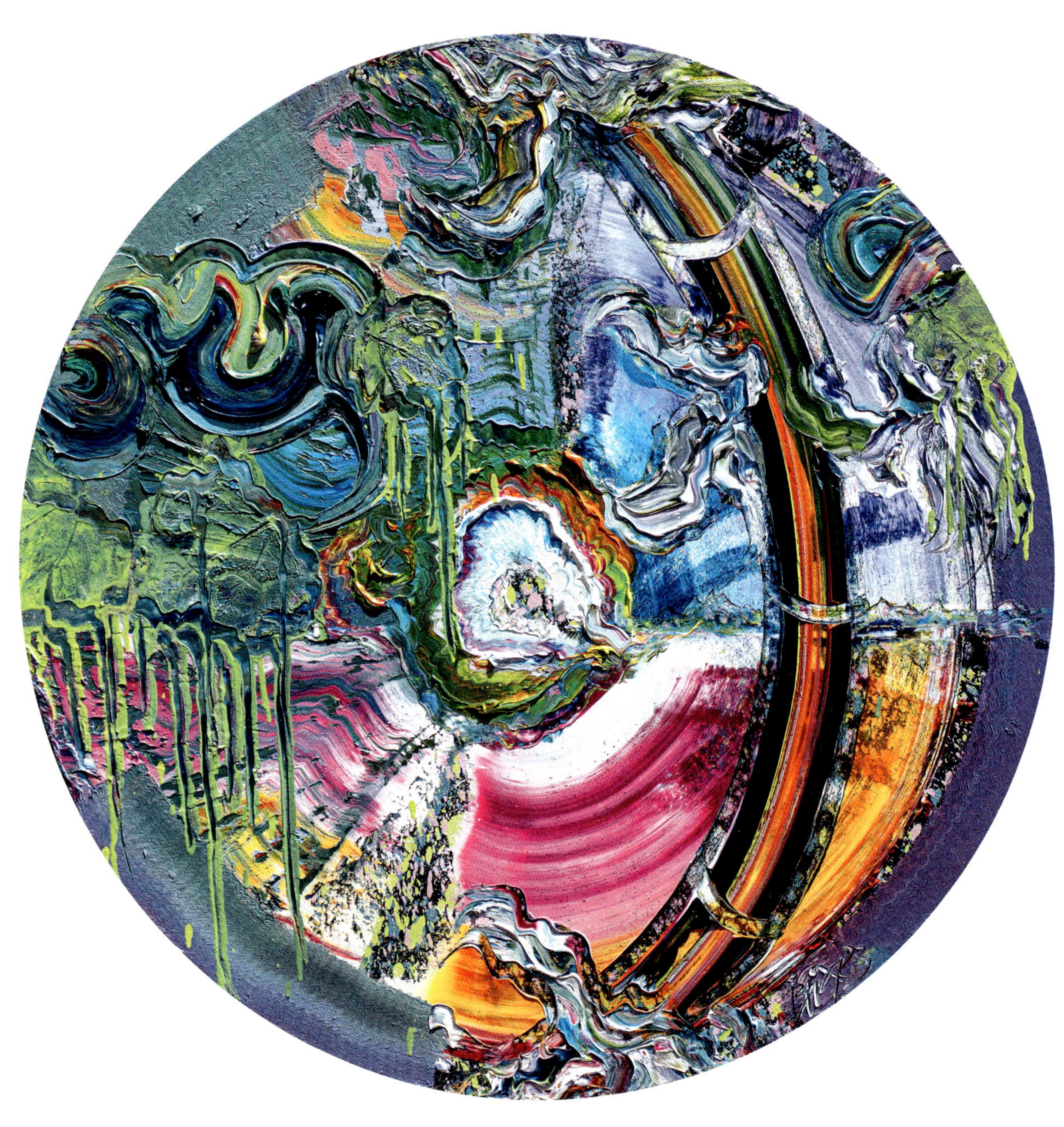

Arise Bamboo Bubble
2023, ø 80 cm

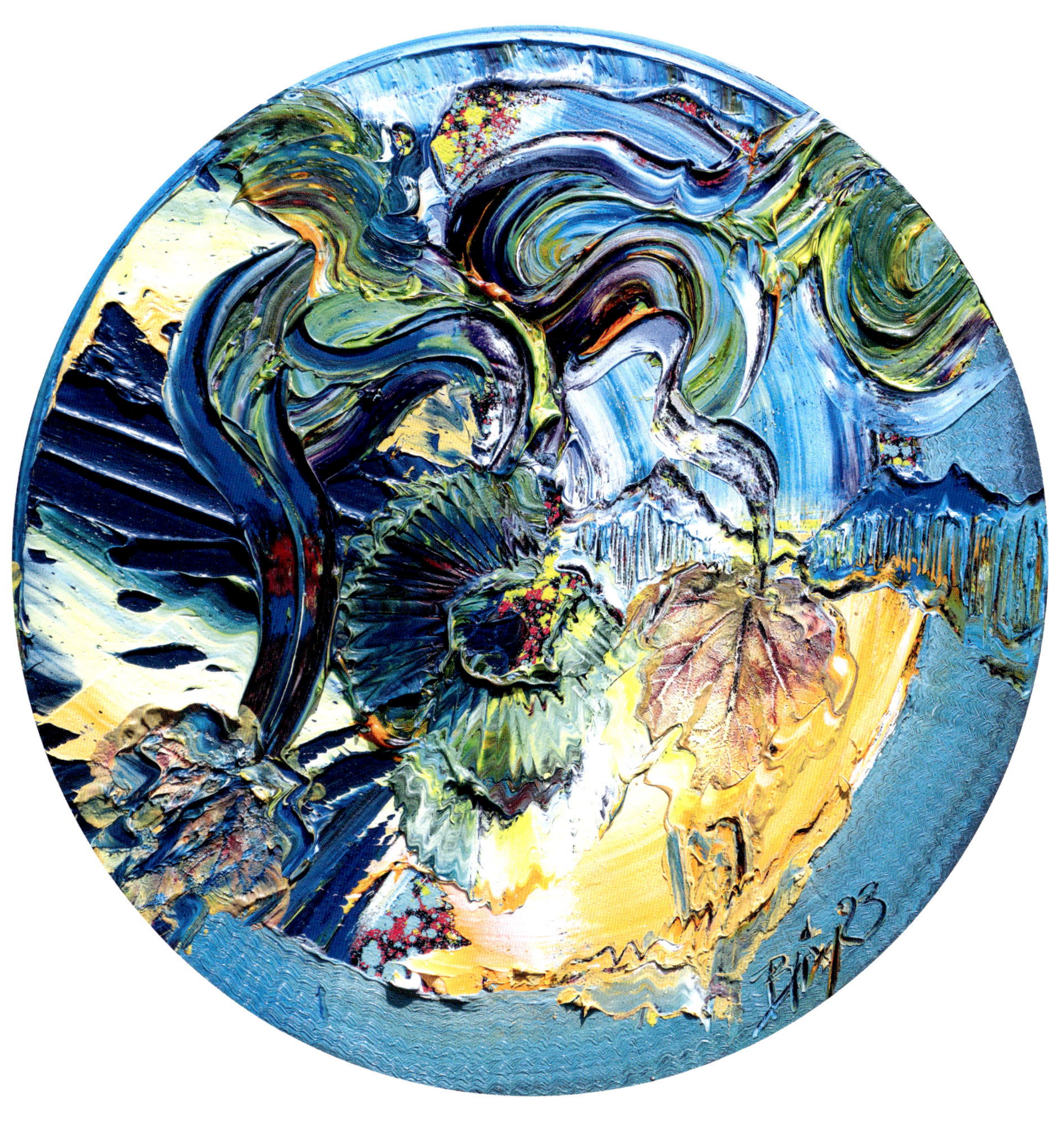

Vishnu Bamboo Bubble
2023, ø 35 cm

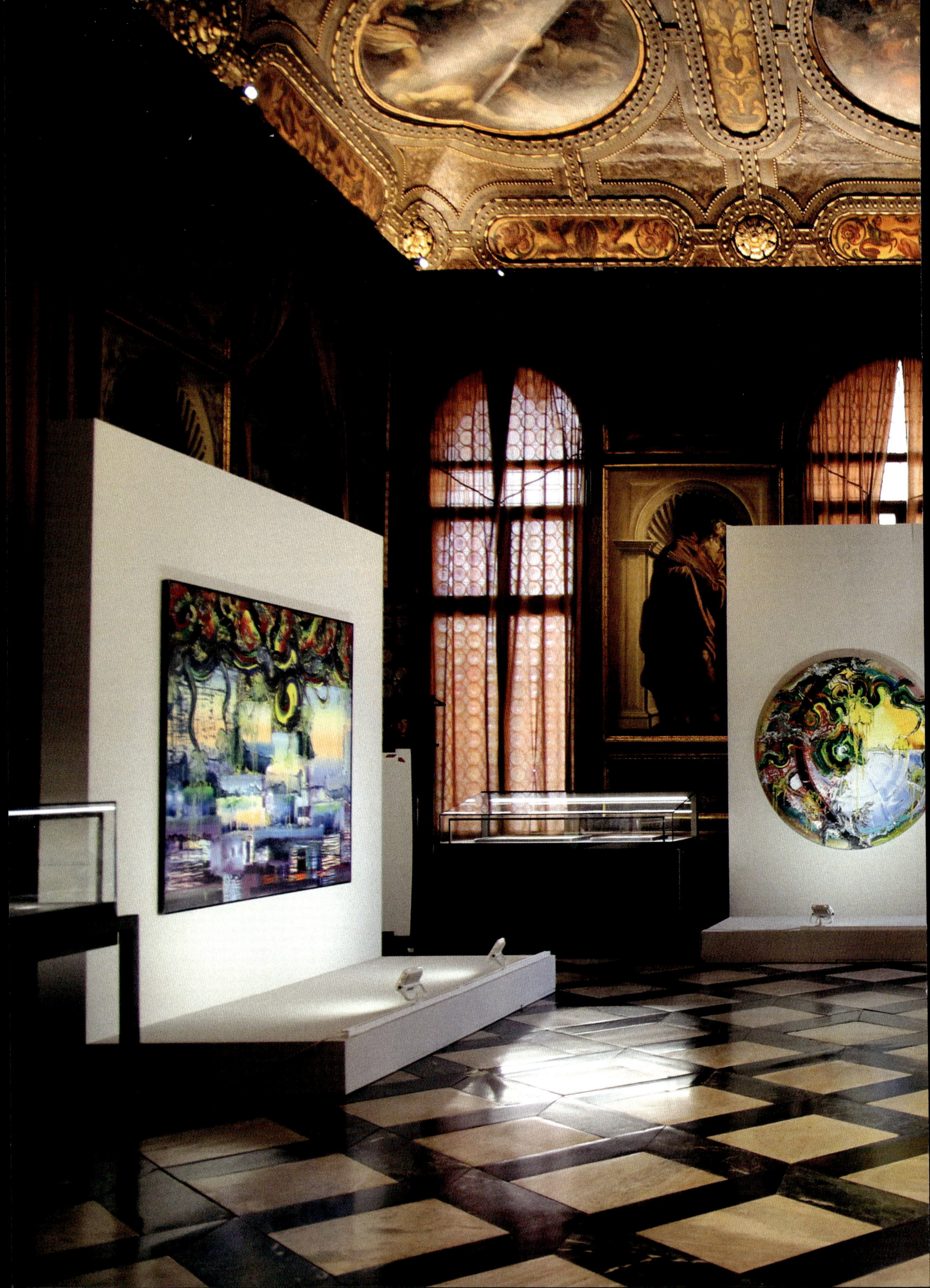

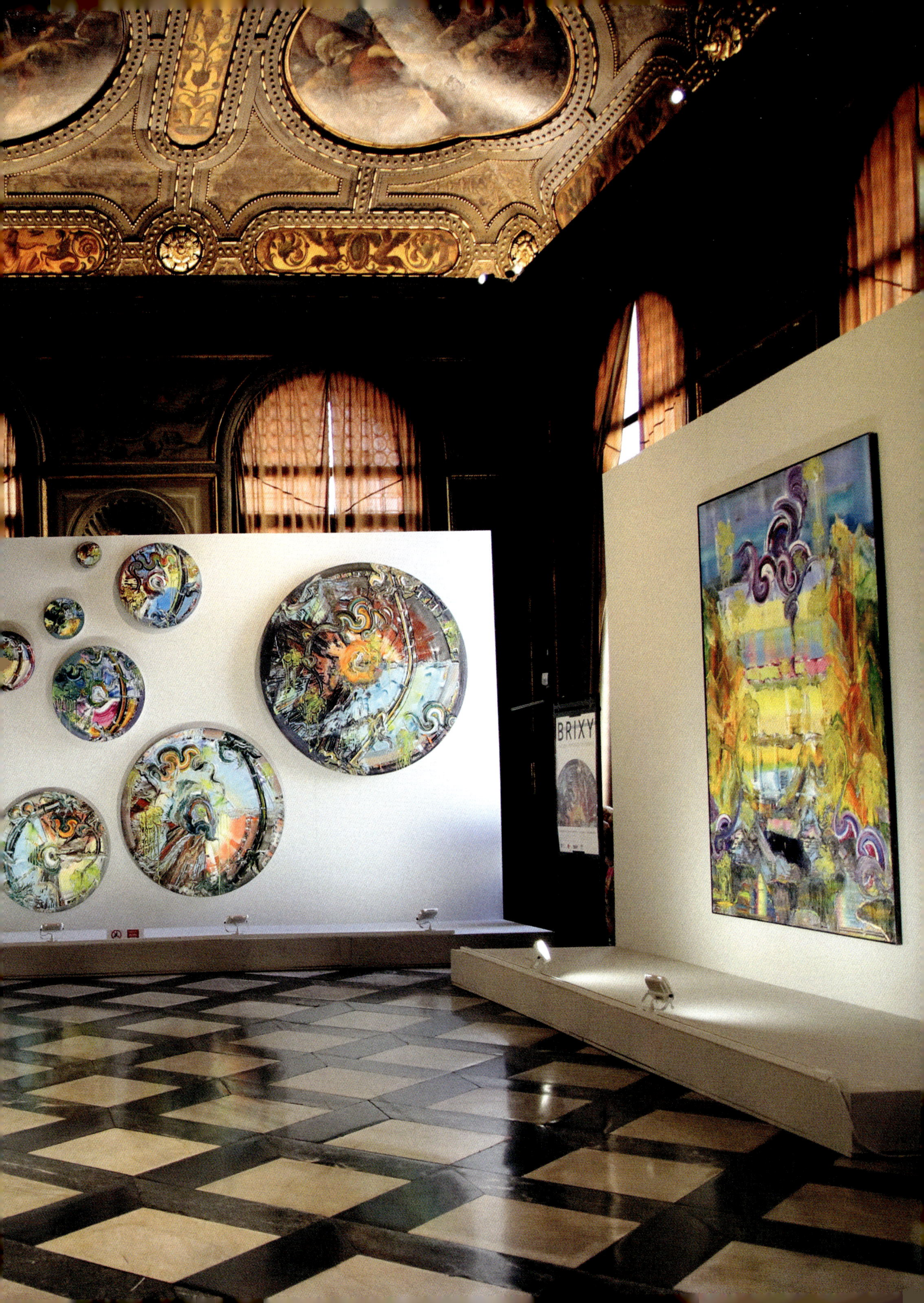
BRIXY

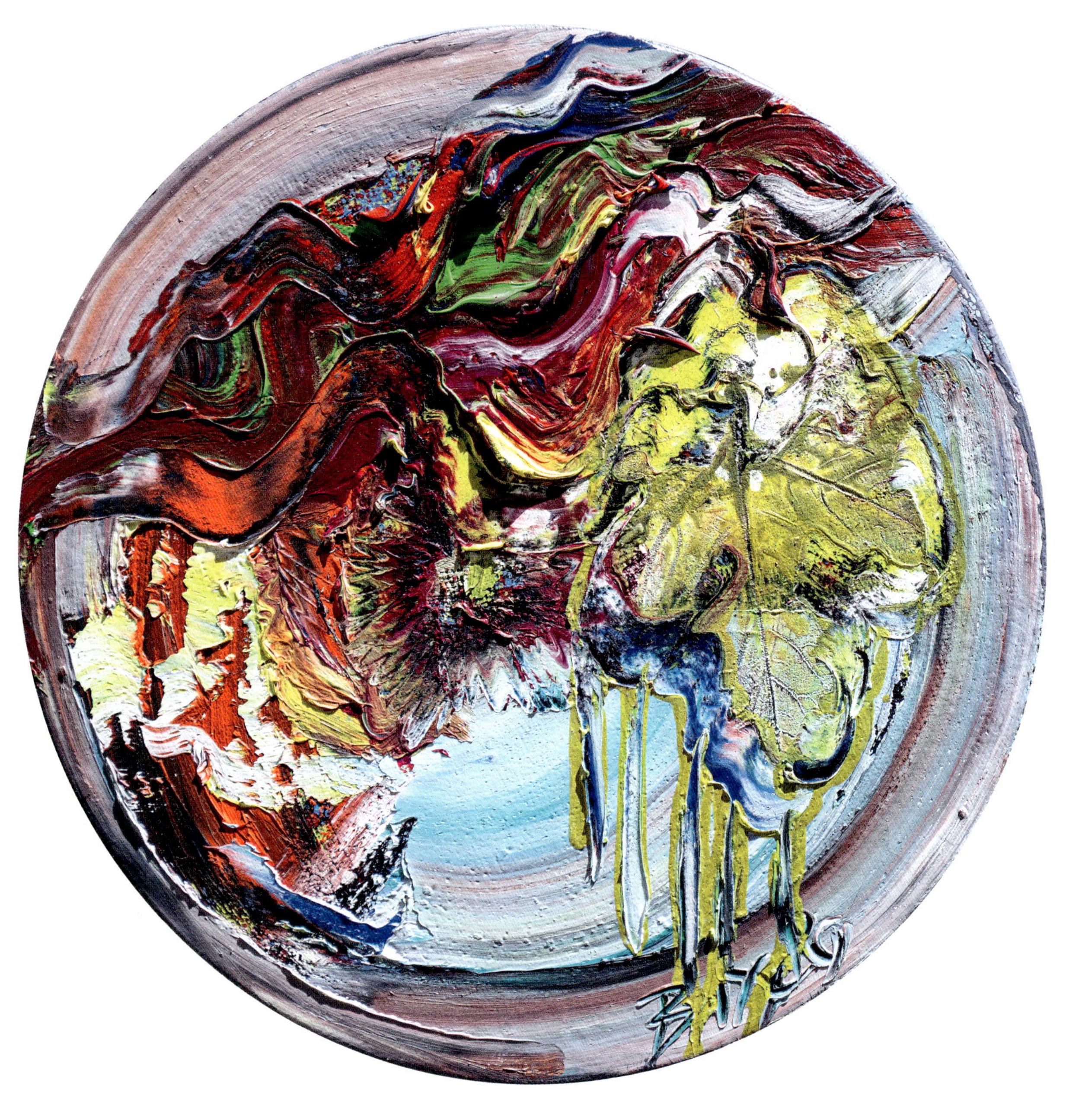

Bite Sized Bamboo Bubble
2020, ø 22 cm

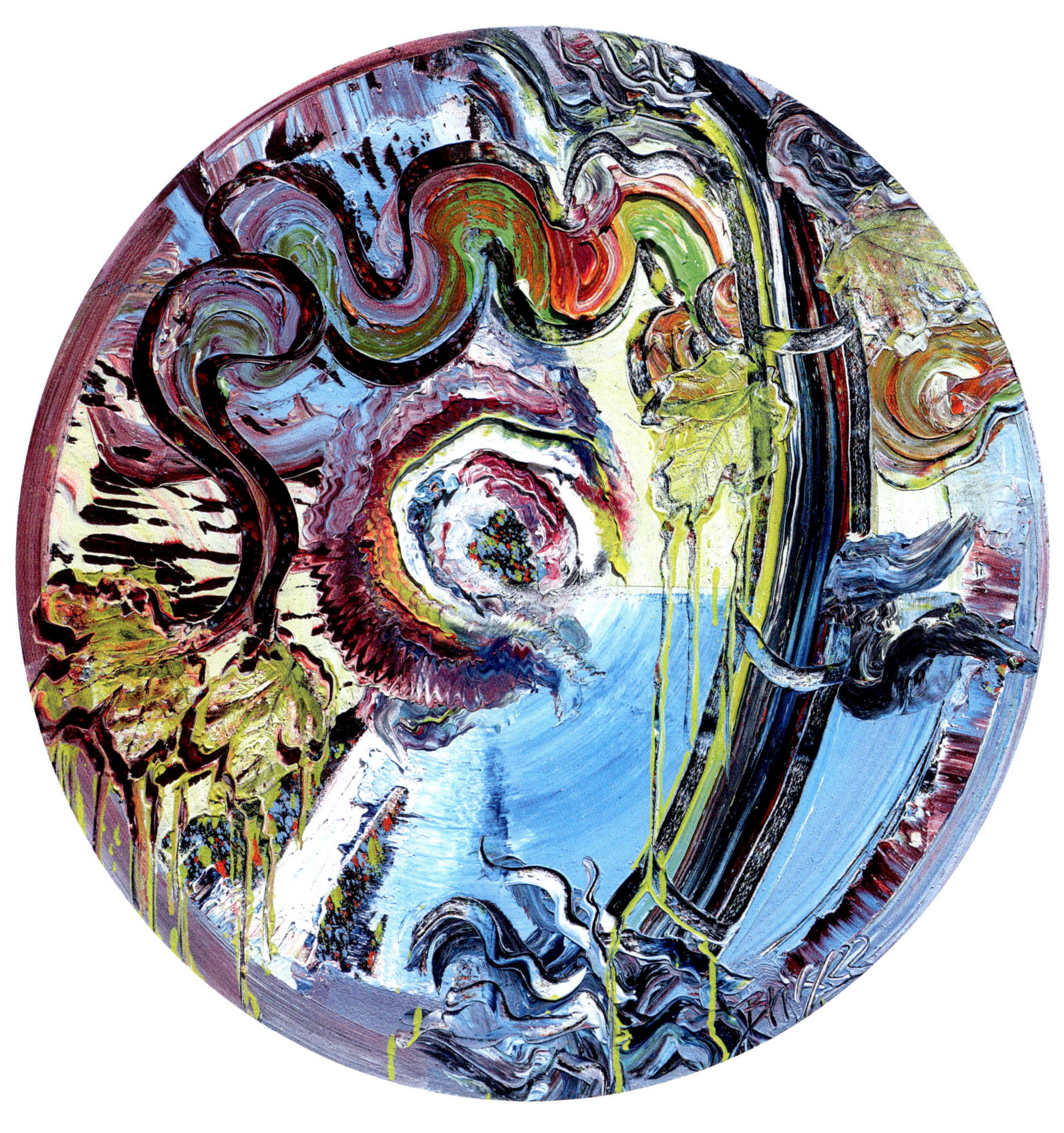

Say Yes Bamboo Bubble
2022, ø 73 cm

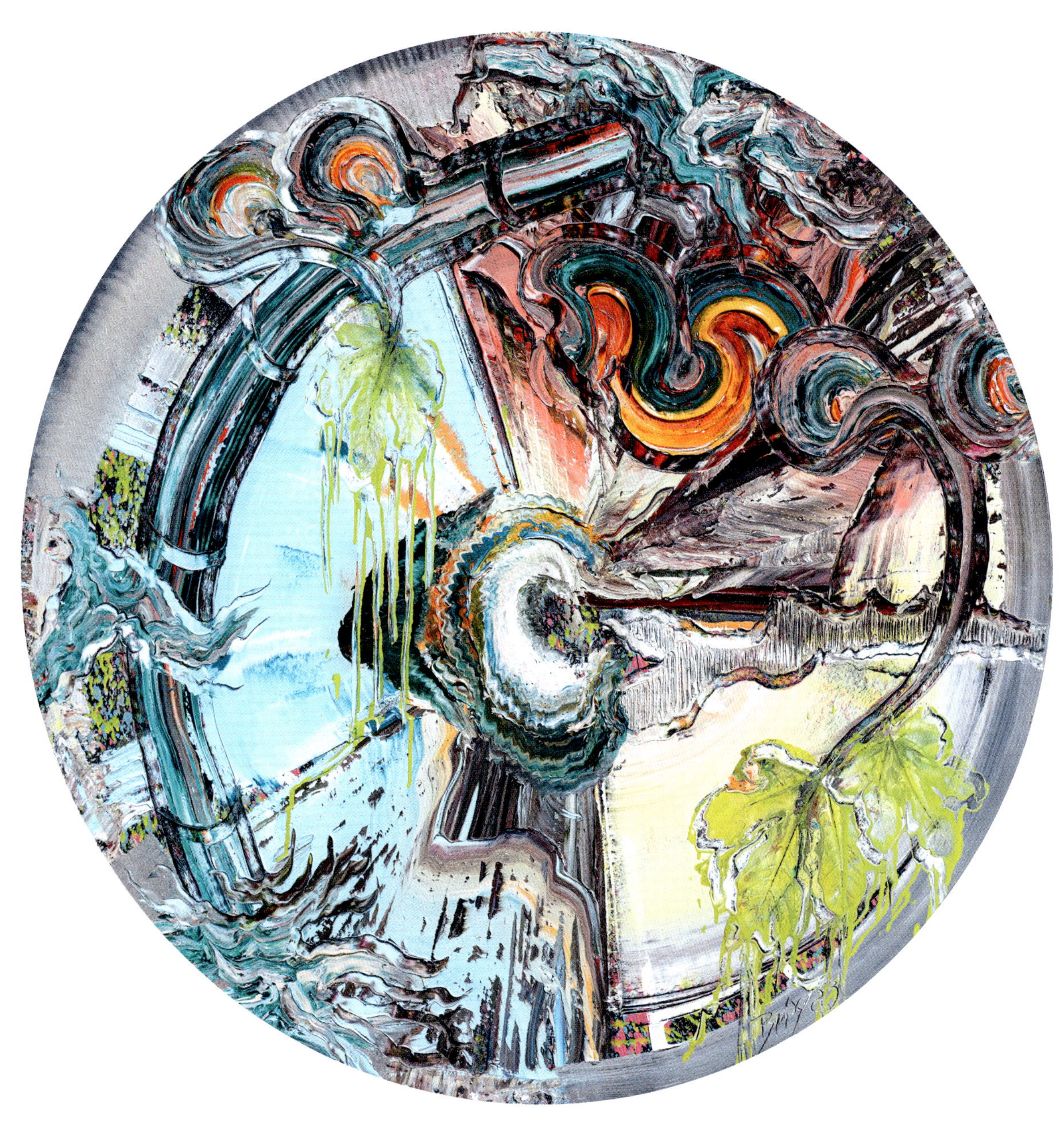

First Steps Bamboo Bubble
2023, ø 100 cm

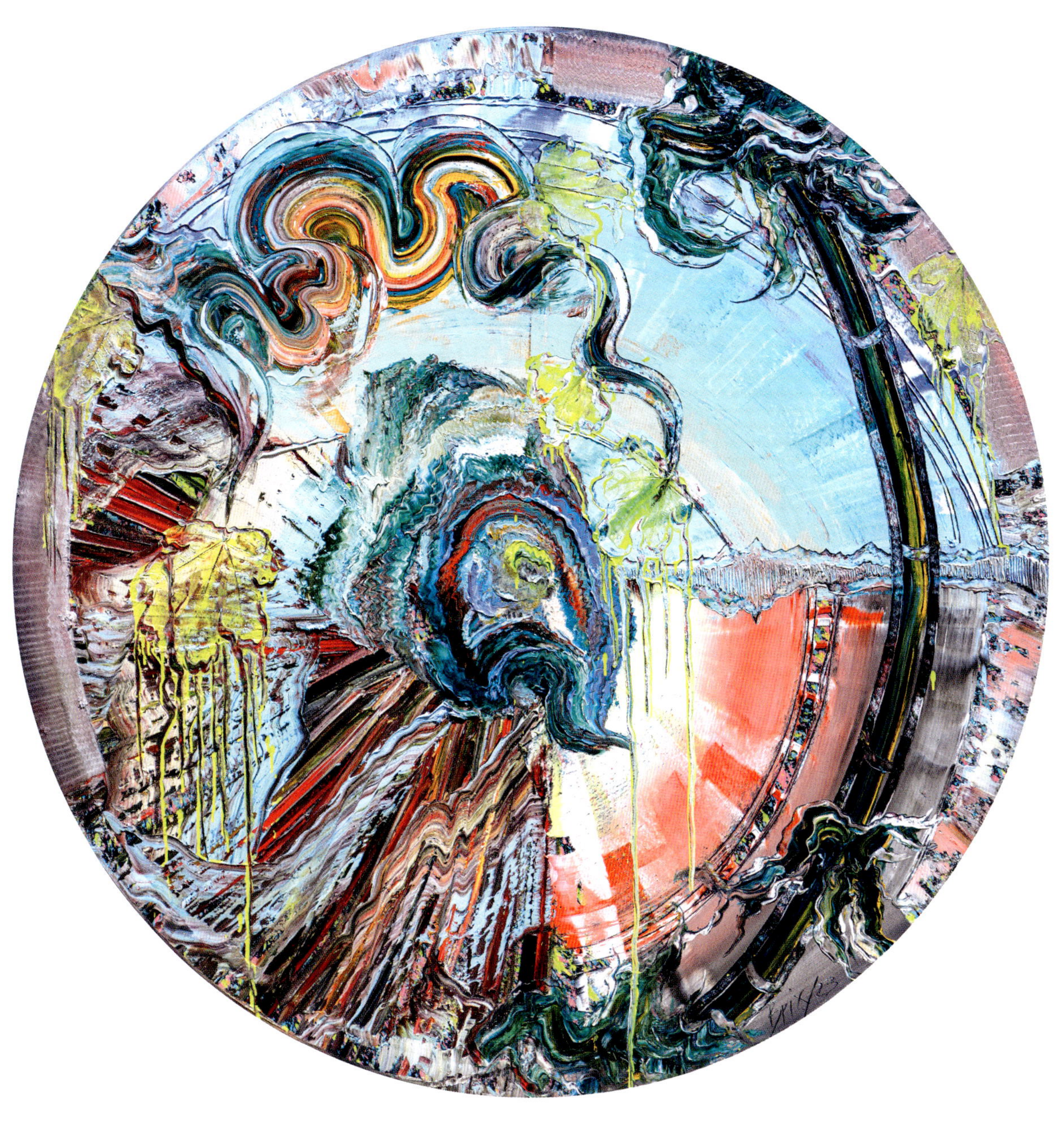

Ascension Bamboo Bubble
2023, ø 140 cm

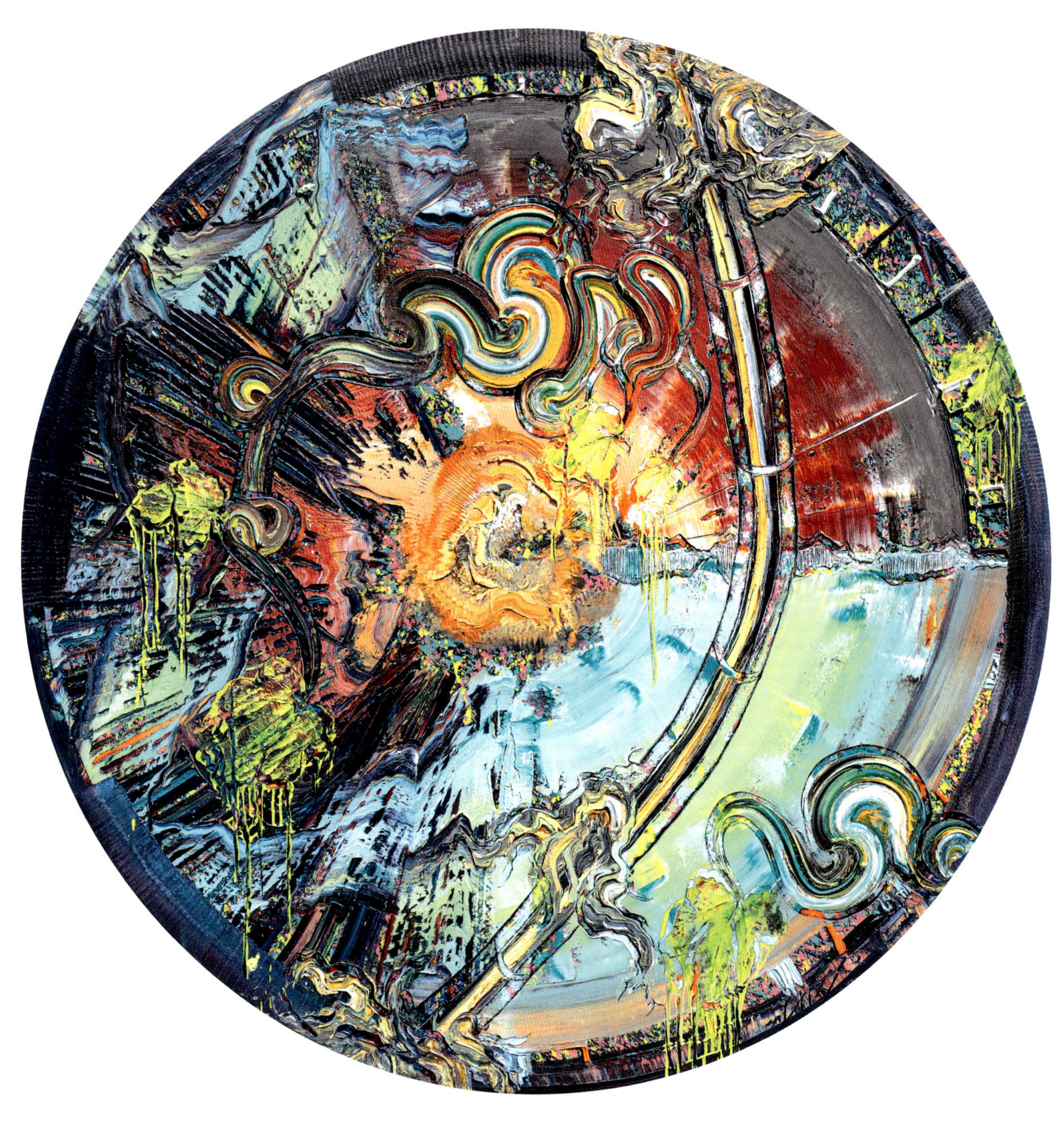

Tapestry Bamboo Bubble
2023, ø 180 cm
S. / p. 57: Detail

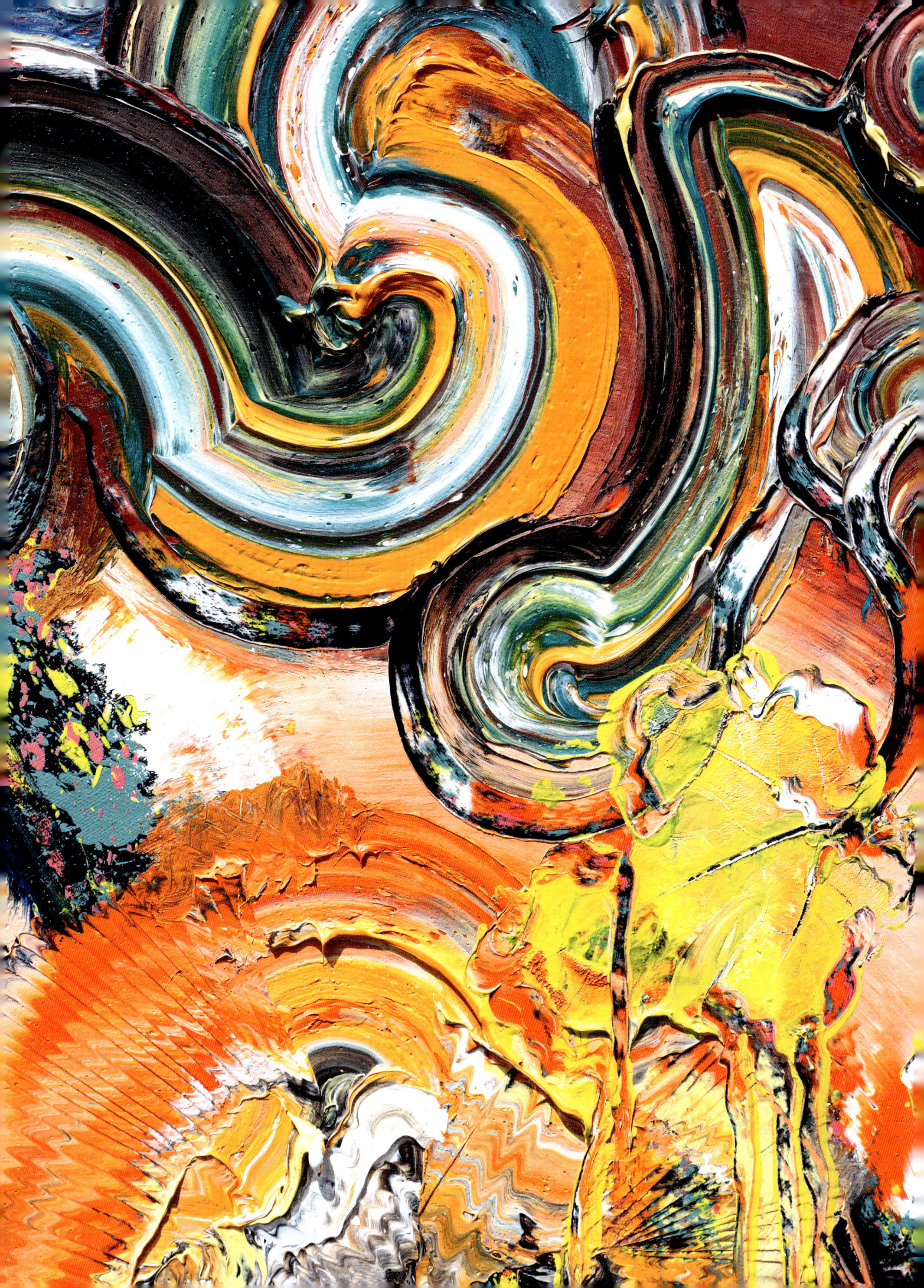

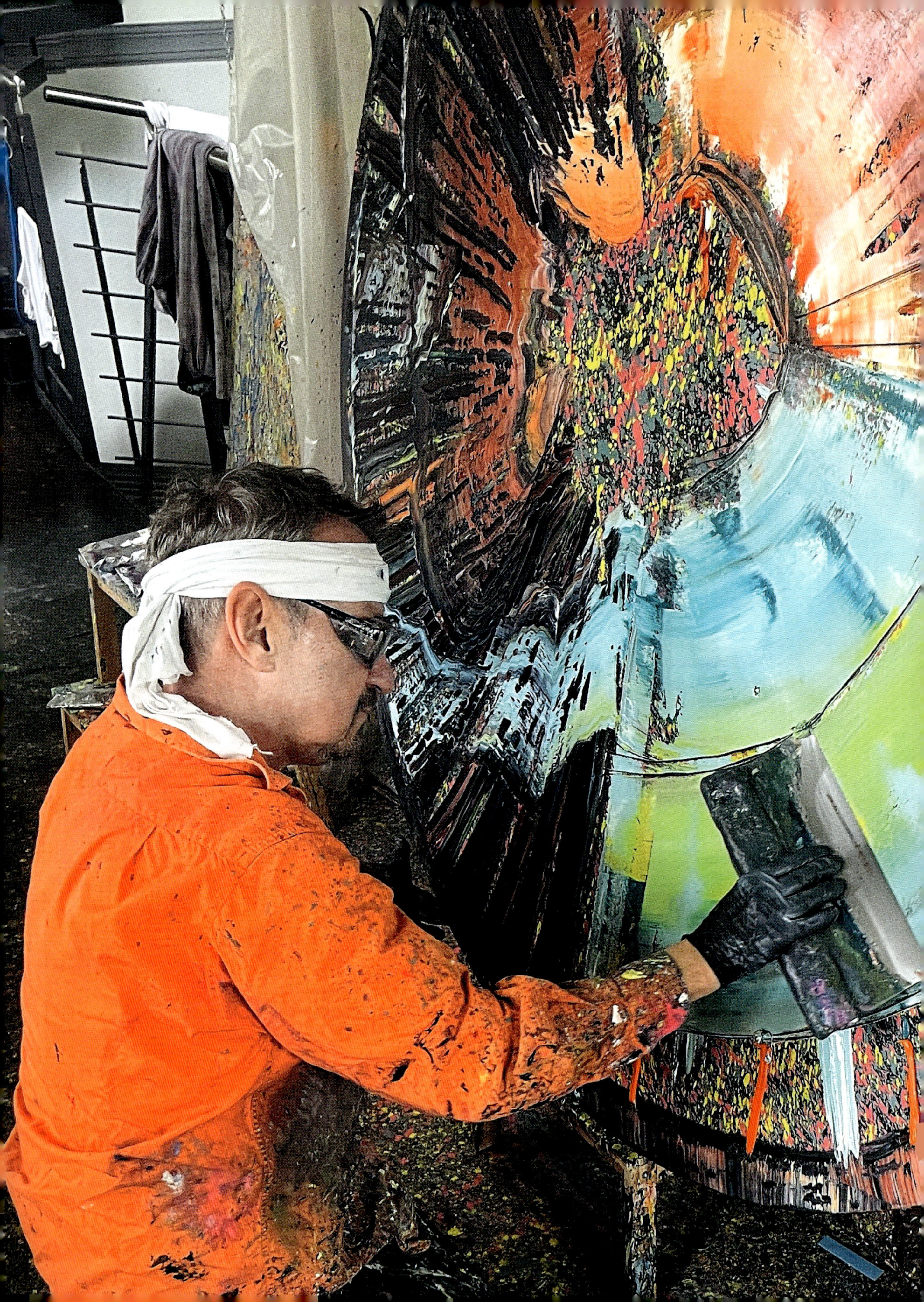

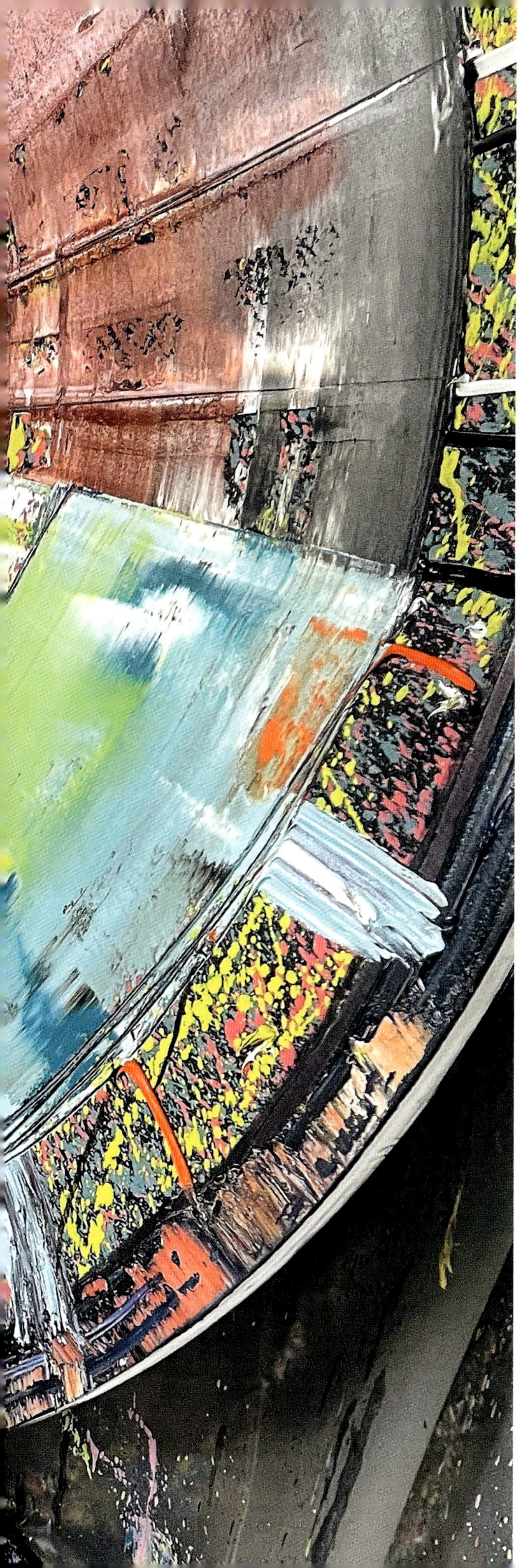

Video:
Entstehungsprozess des /
Creation Process of
Tapestry Bamboo Bubble
2023, ø 180 cm

»DIE FEIGENBLÄTTER IN MEINEN BILDERN SIND SYMBOLE DER VERBINDUNG ZWISCHEN REALER NATUR UND ABSTRAKTER LANDSCHAFT, EINE BRÜCKE ZWISCHEN ZWEI WELTEN.«

»THE FIG LEAVES IN MY PAINTINGS ARE SYMBOLS OF THE CONNECTION BETWEEN REAL NATURE AND ABSTRACT LANDSCAPE, A BRIDGE BETWEEN TWO WORLDS.«

Dietmar Brixy

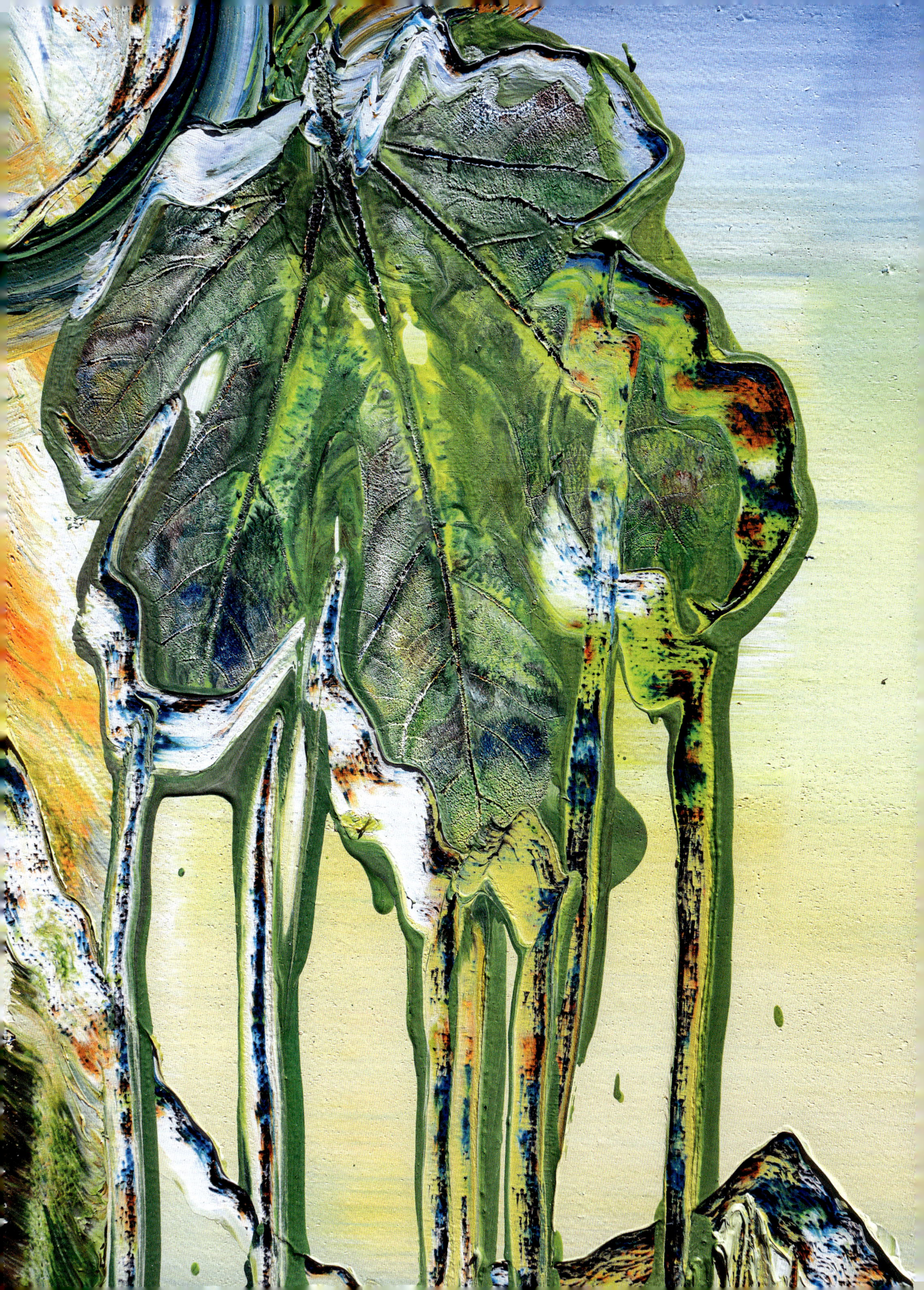

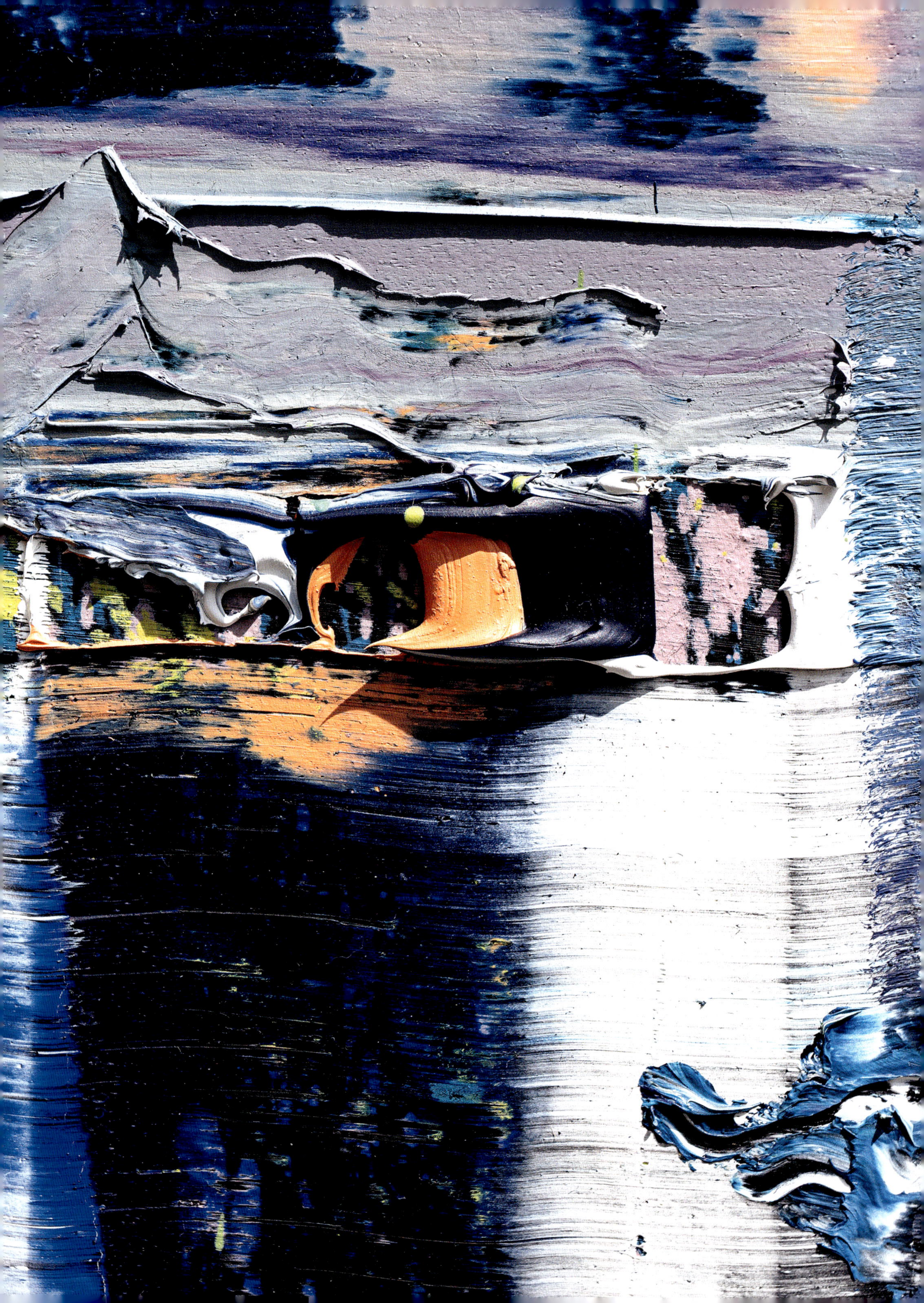

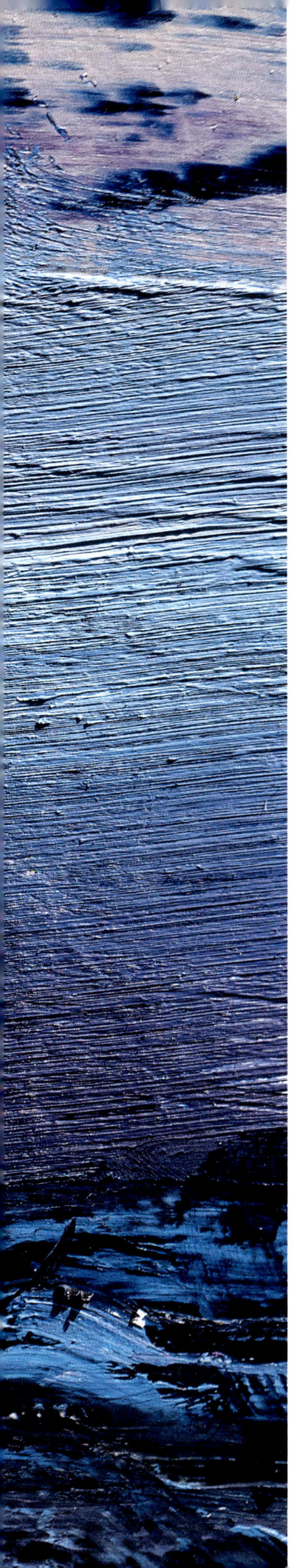

MALEREI

PAINTINGS

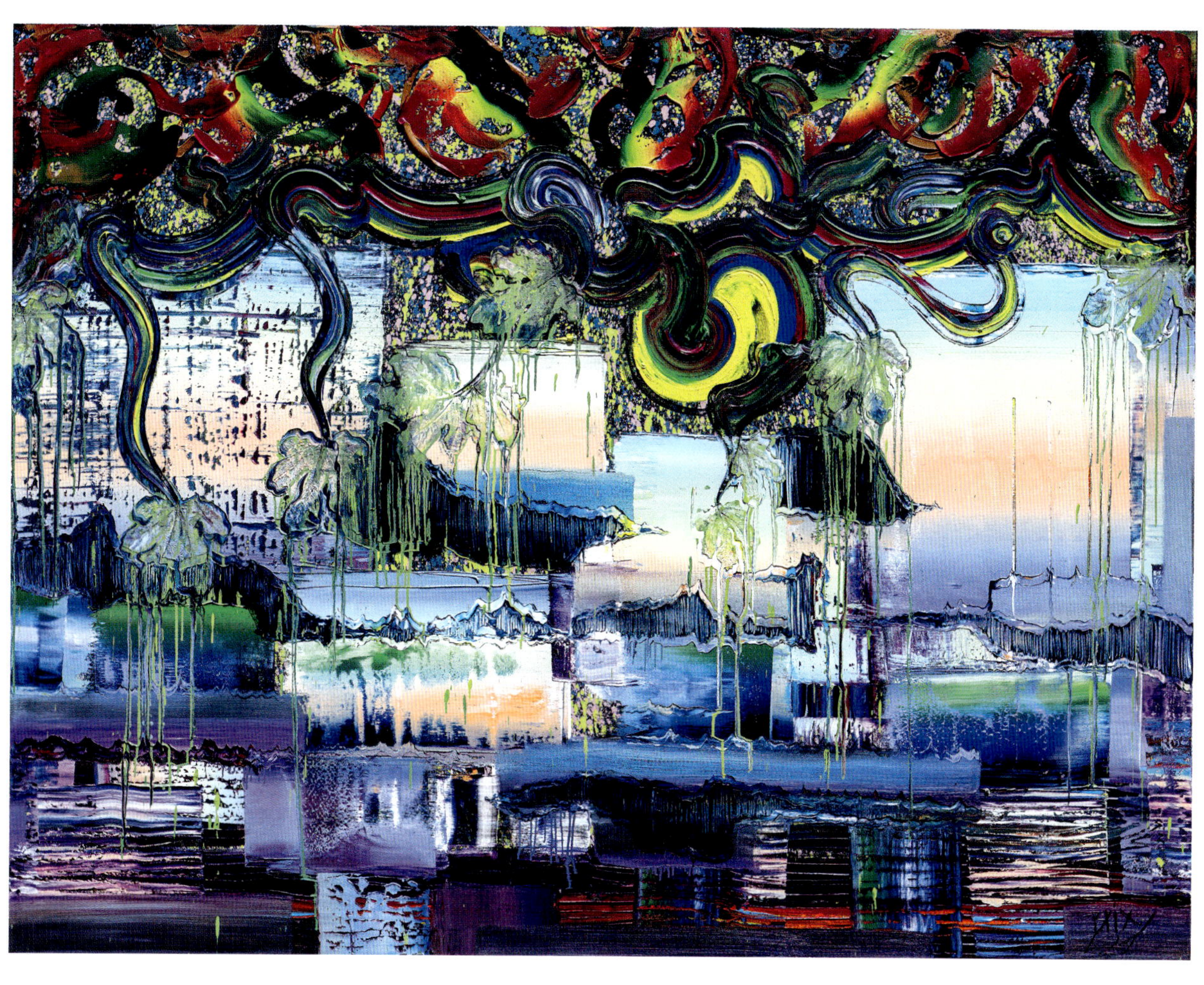

Happy
2021, 160 × 210 cm

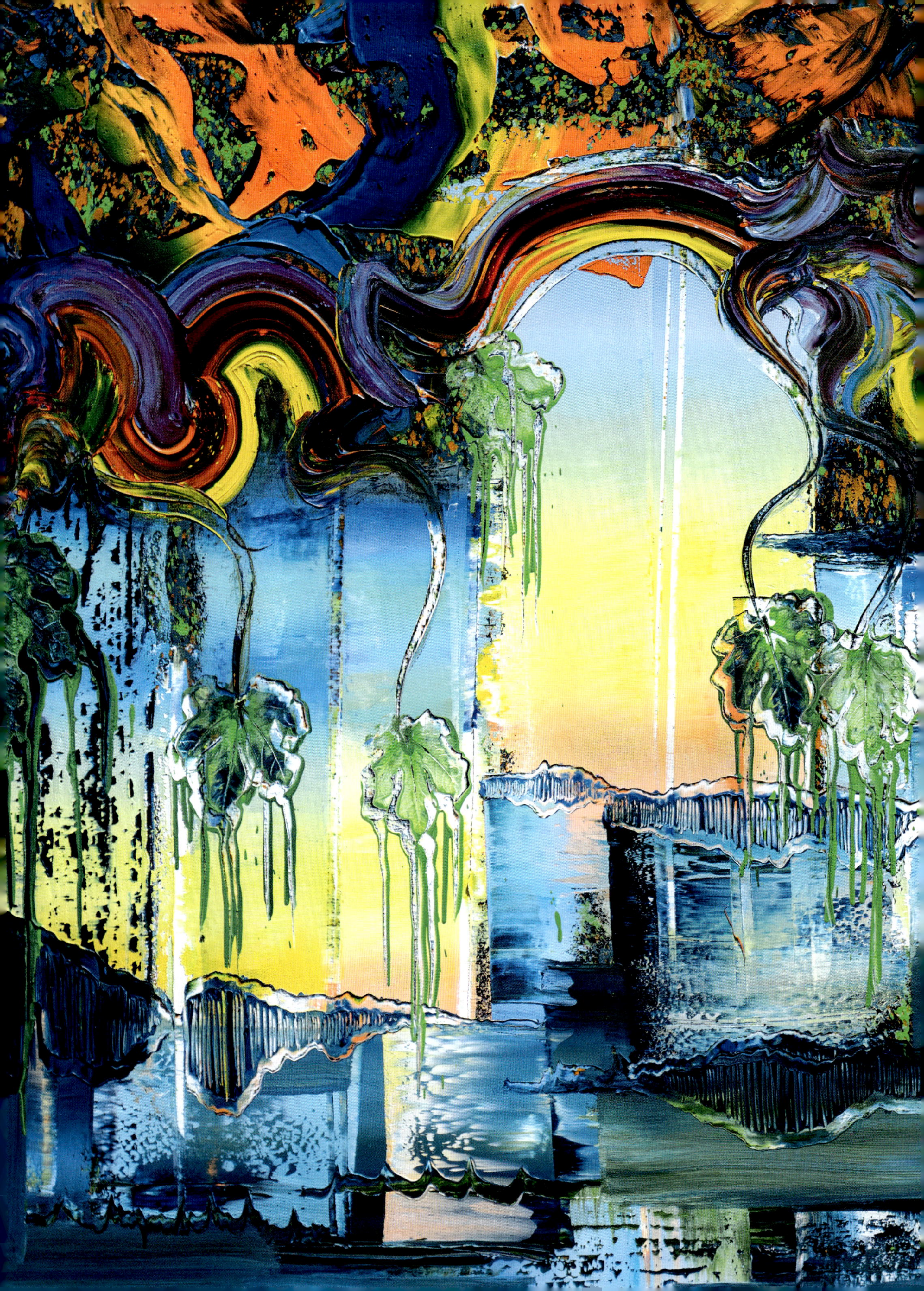

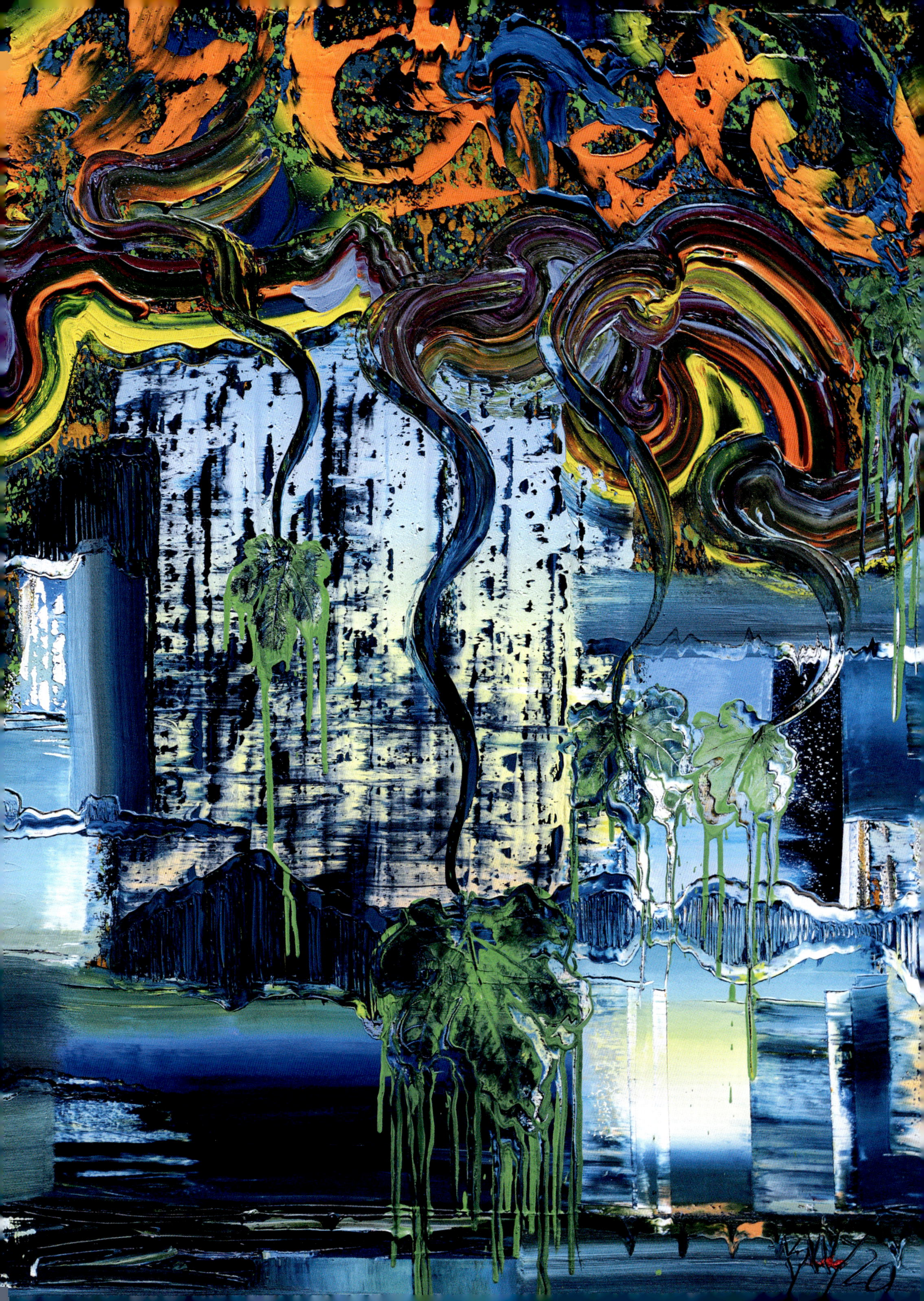

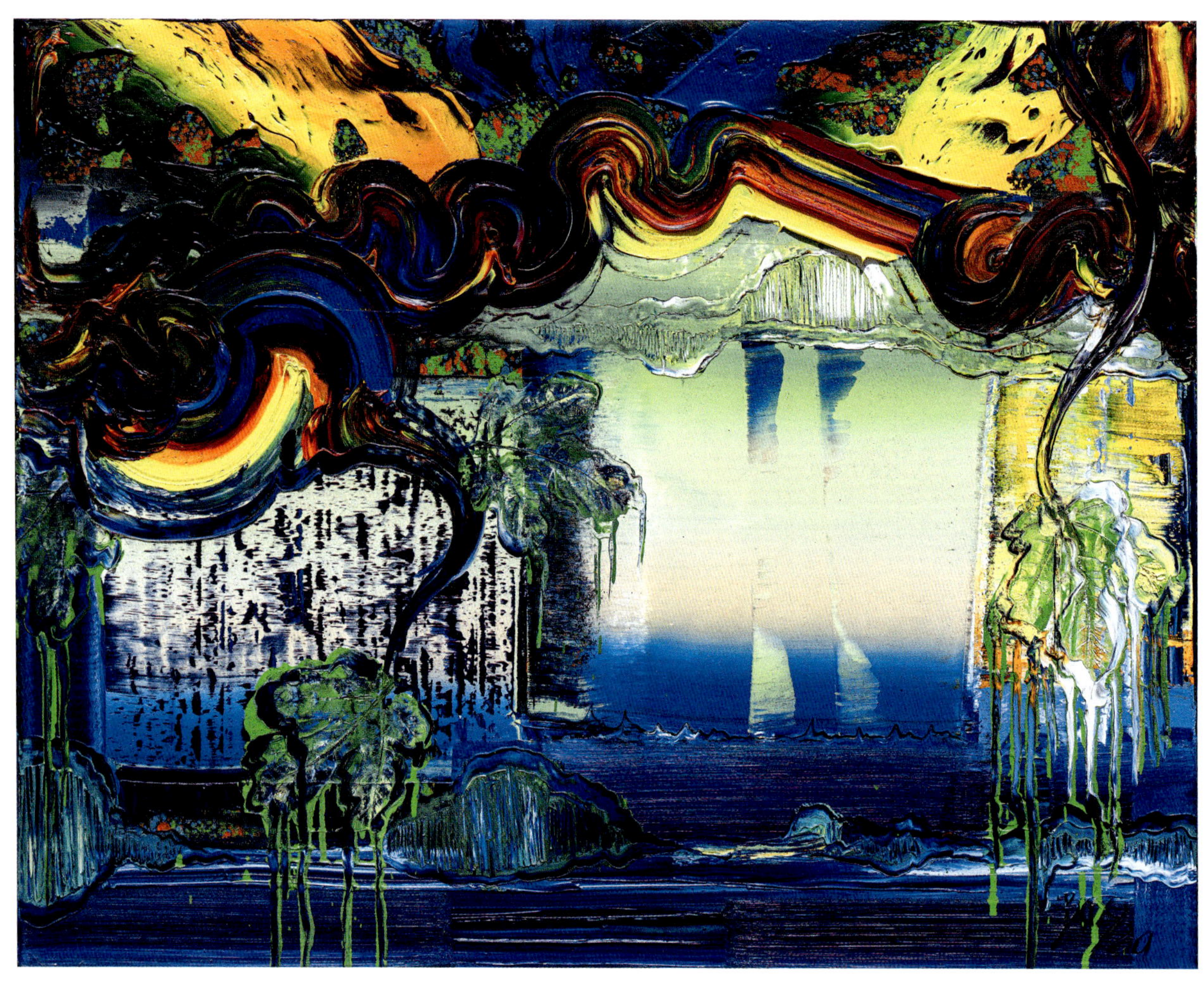

S. / pp. 66/67:
Happy
2020, 120 × 180 cm

Happy
2020, 70 × 90 cm

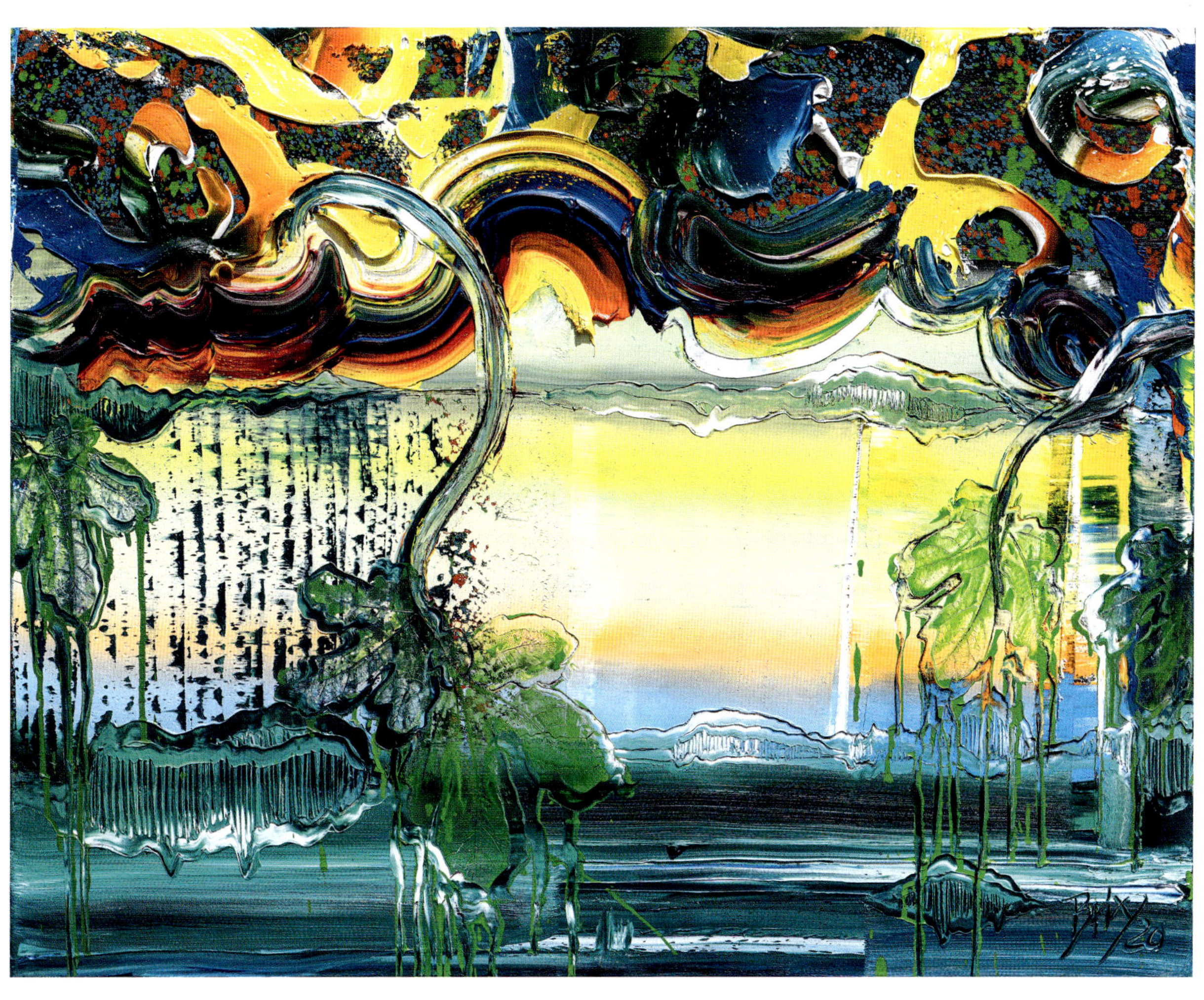

Happy
2020, 70 × 90 cm

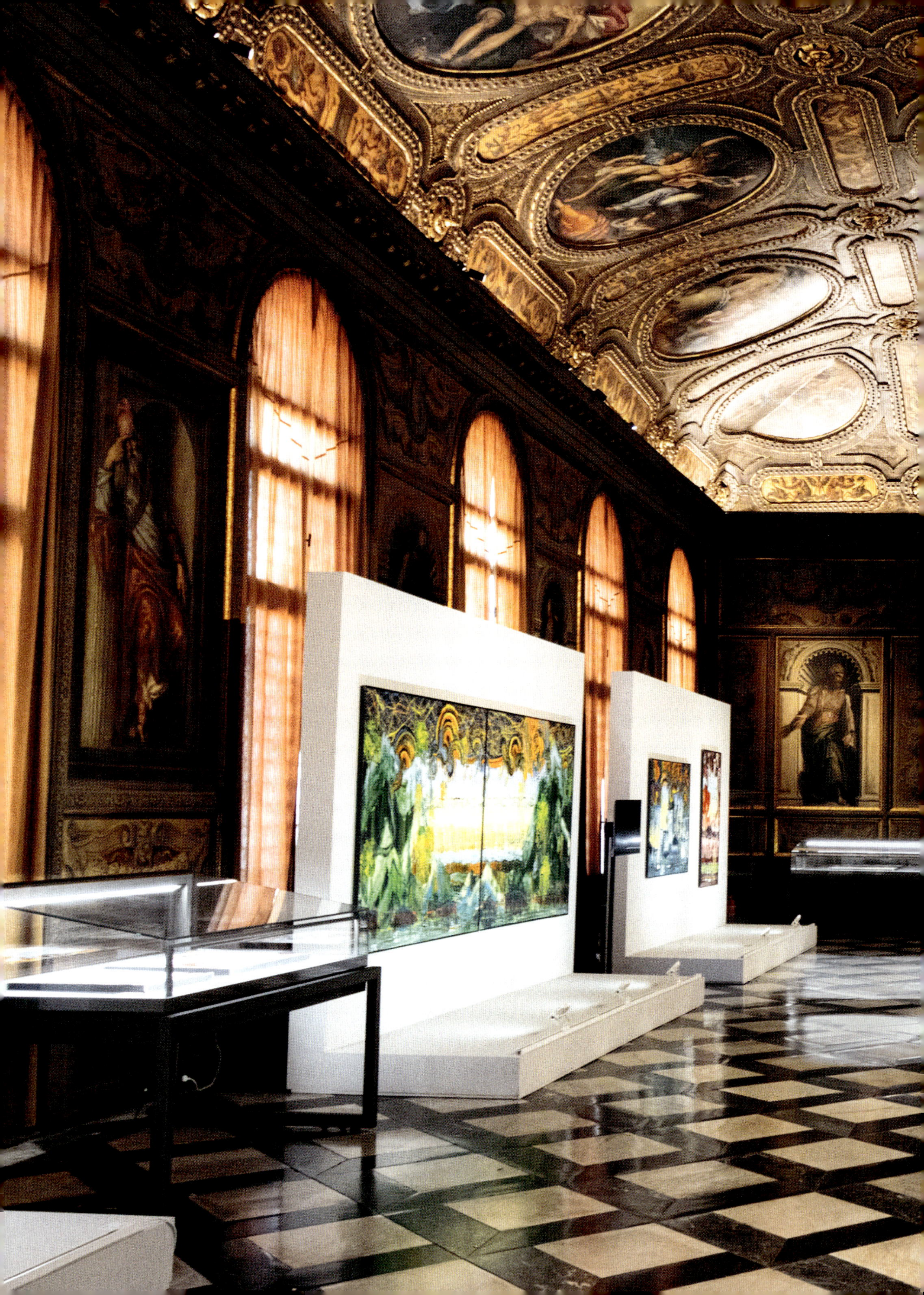

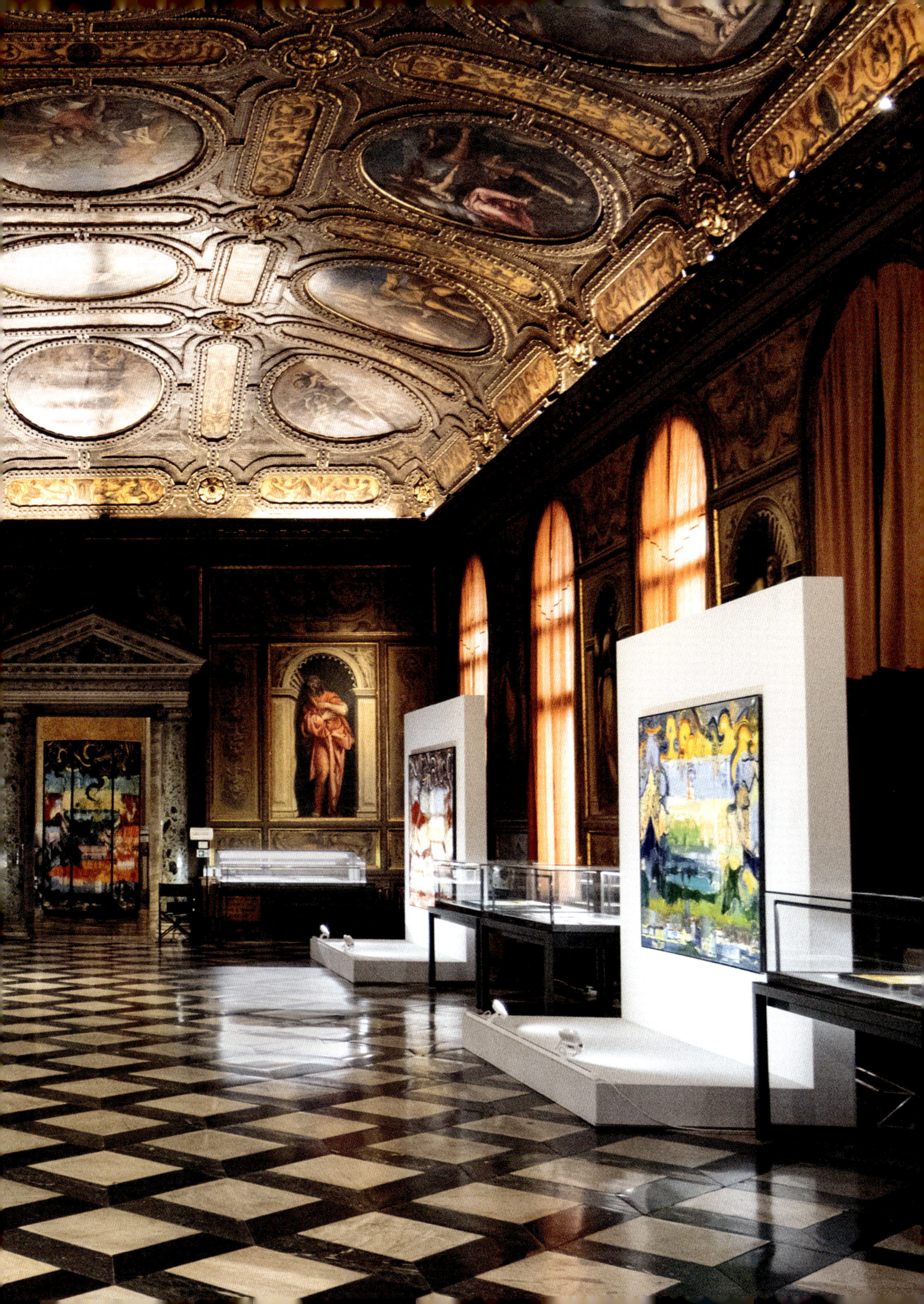

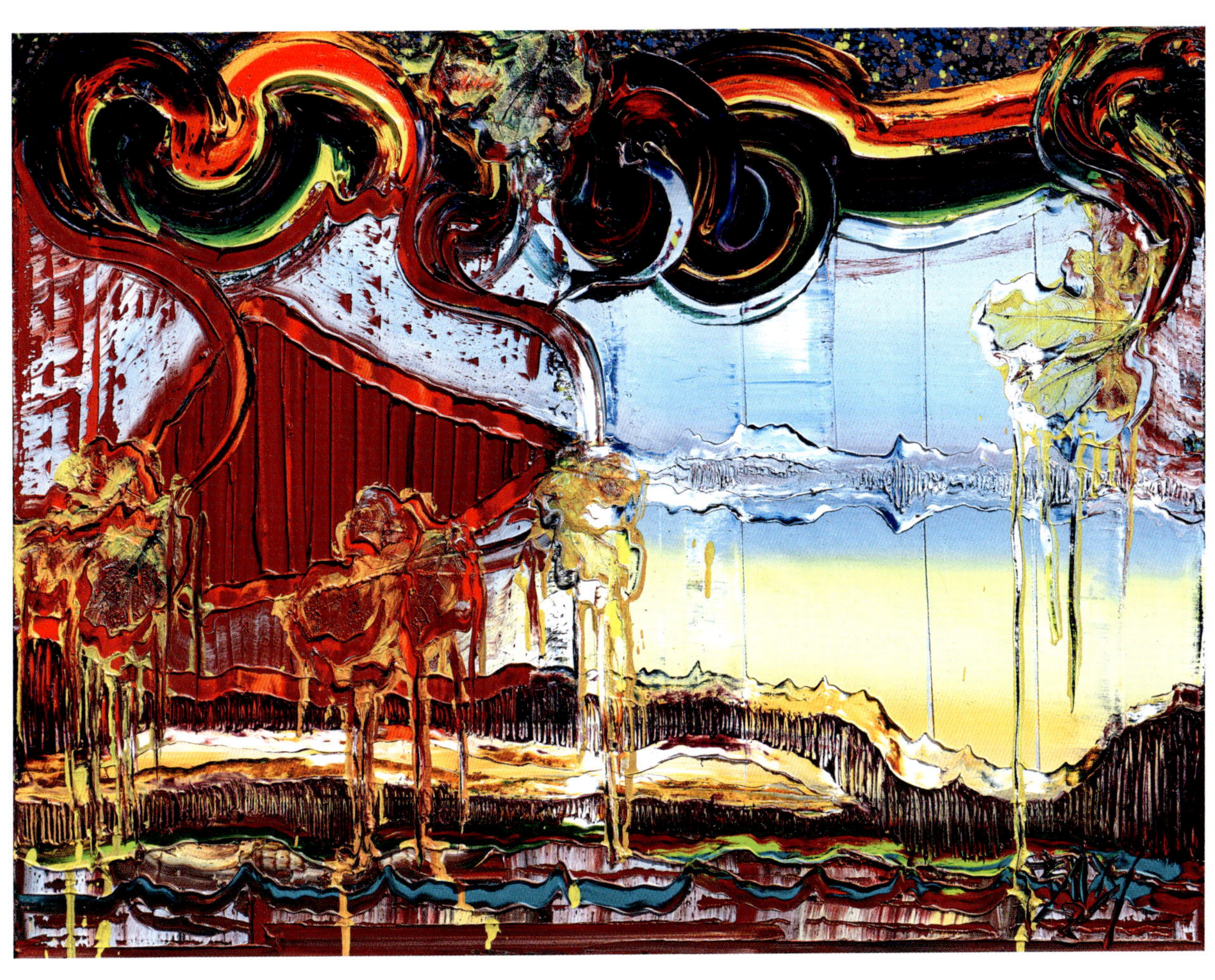

Reflect
2021, 60 × 80 cm

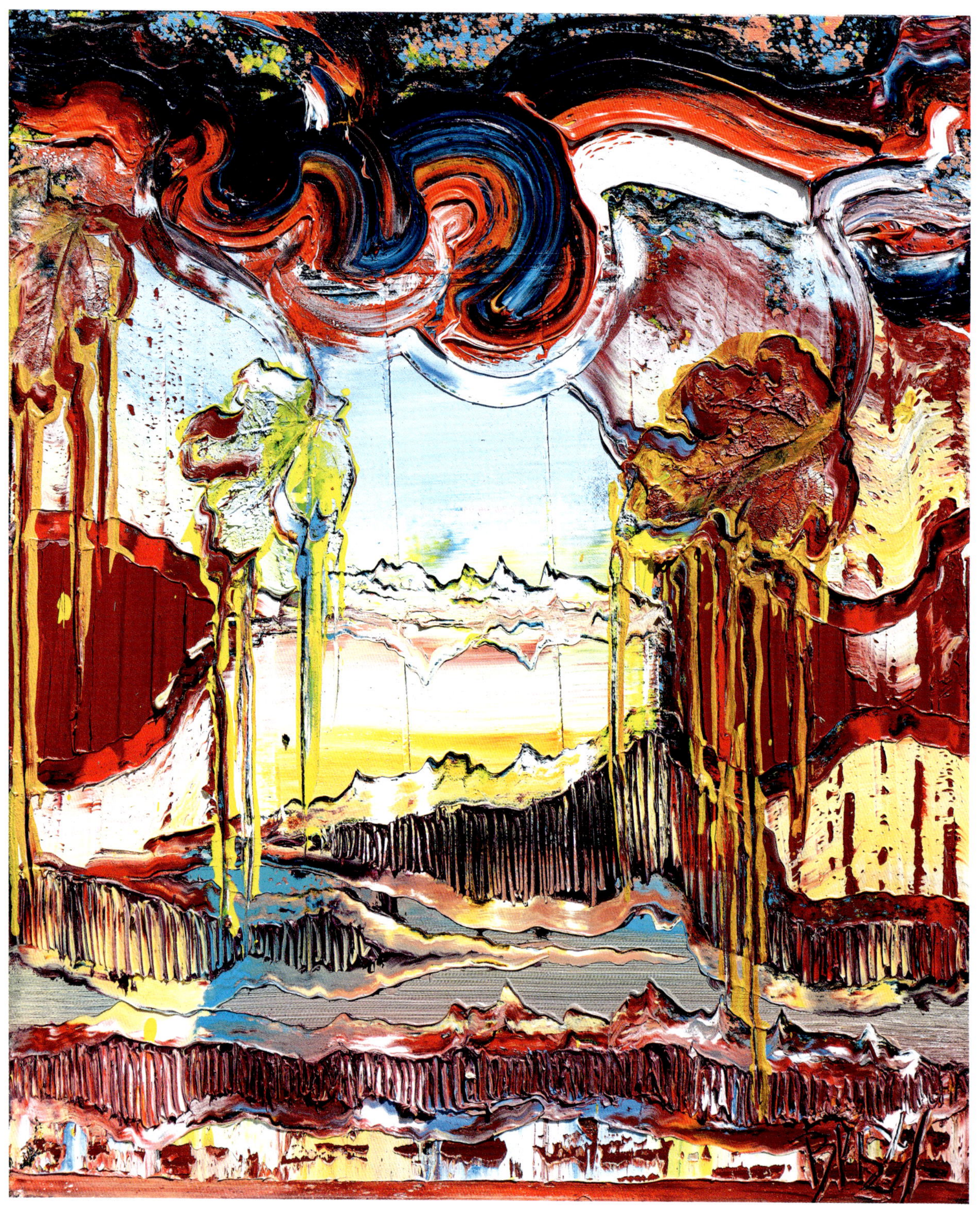

Reflect
2021, 60 × 50 cm

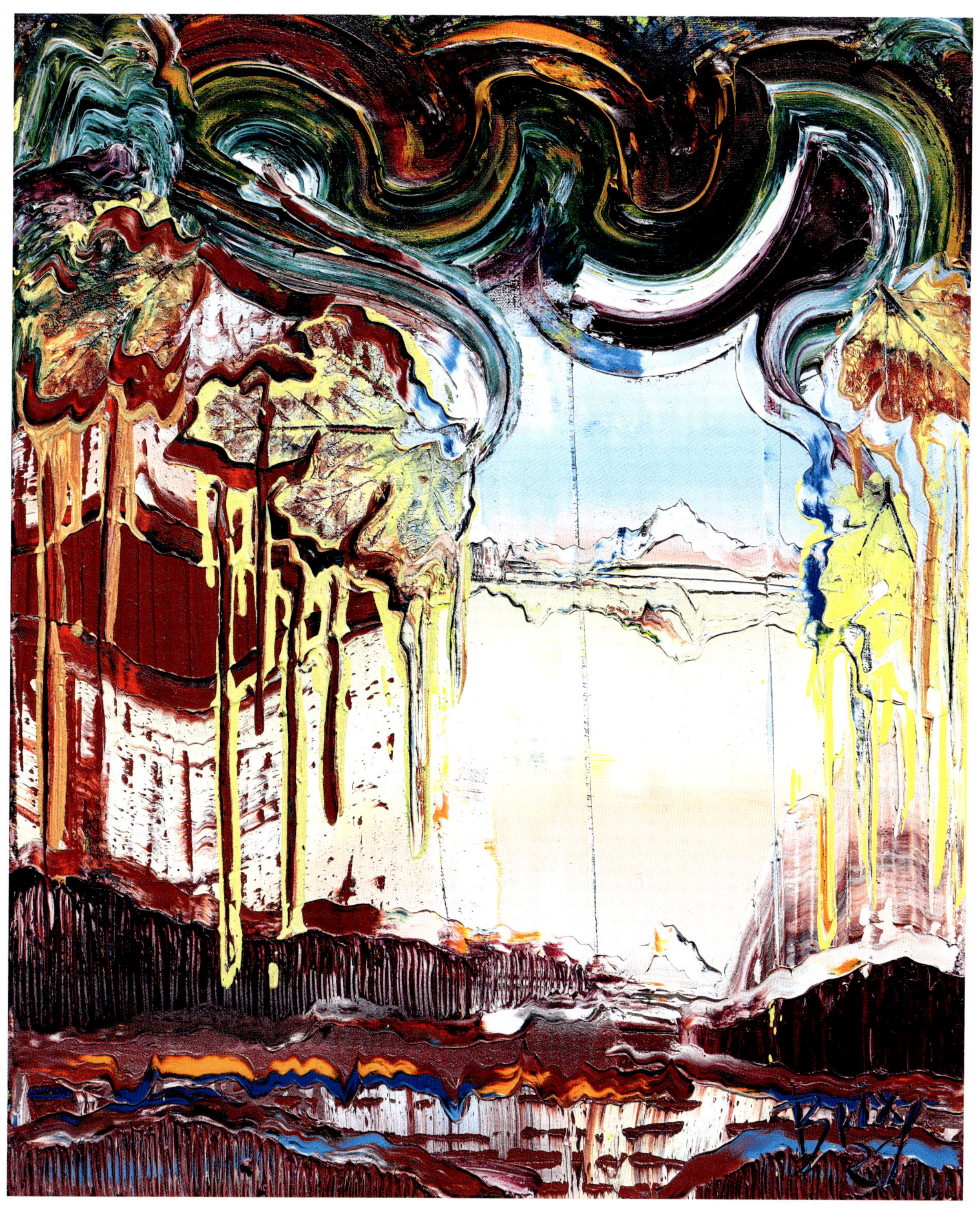

Reflect
2021, 60 × 50 cm

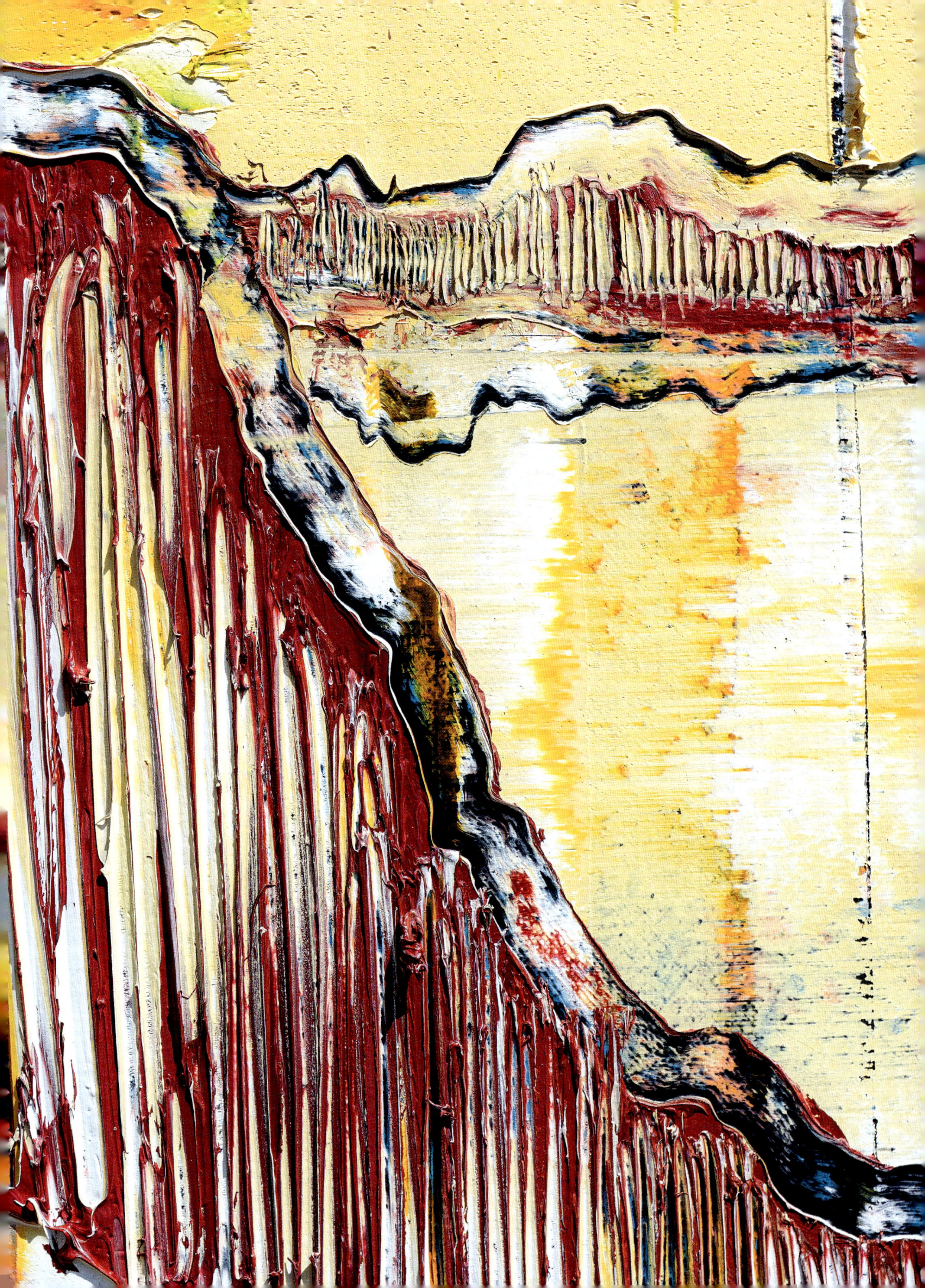

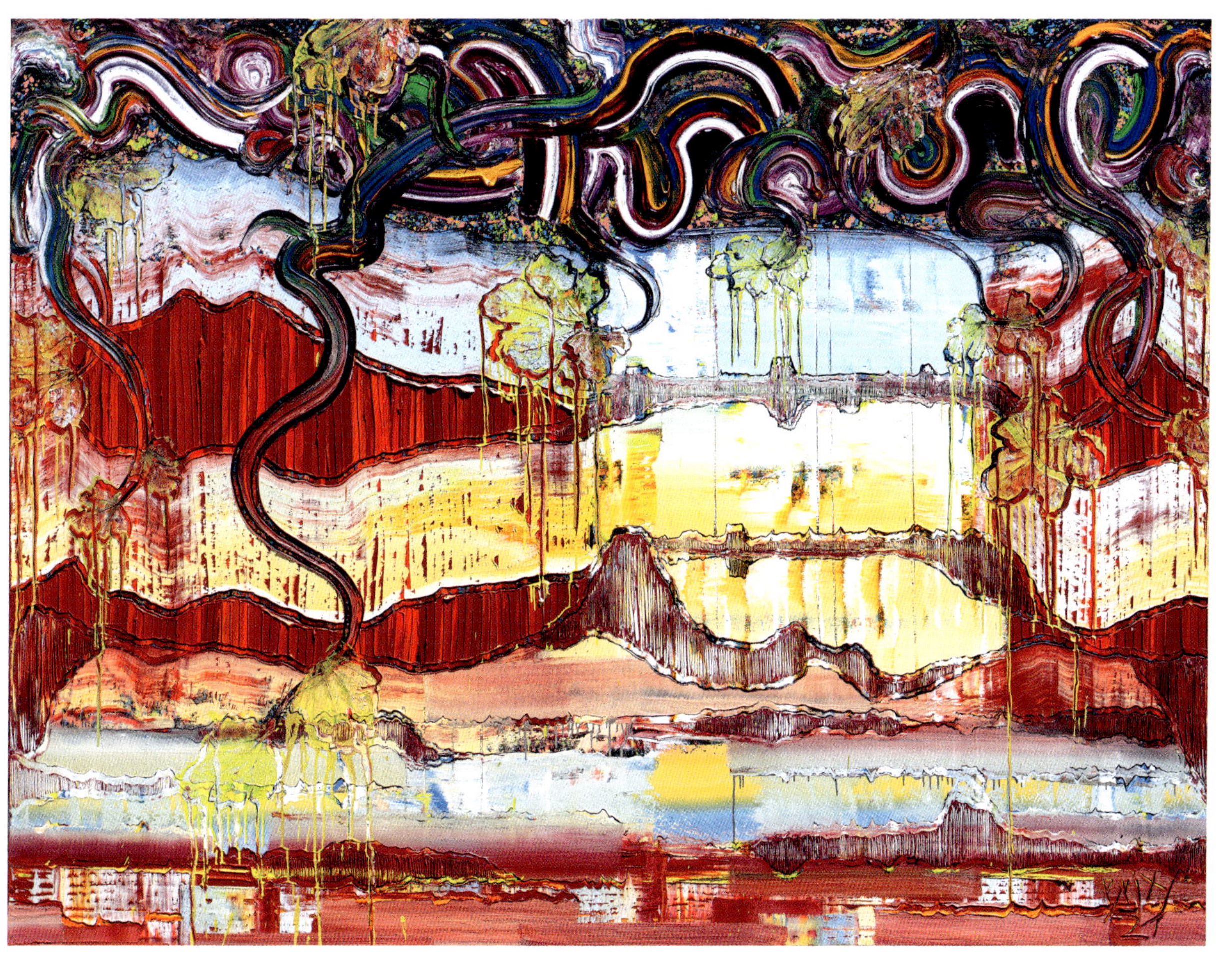

Reflect
2021, 180 × 240 cm
Links / left: Detail

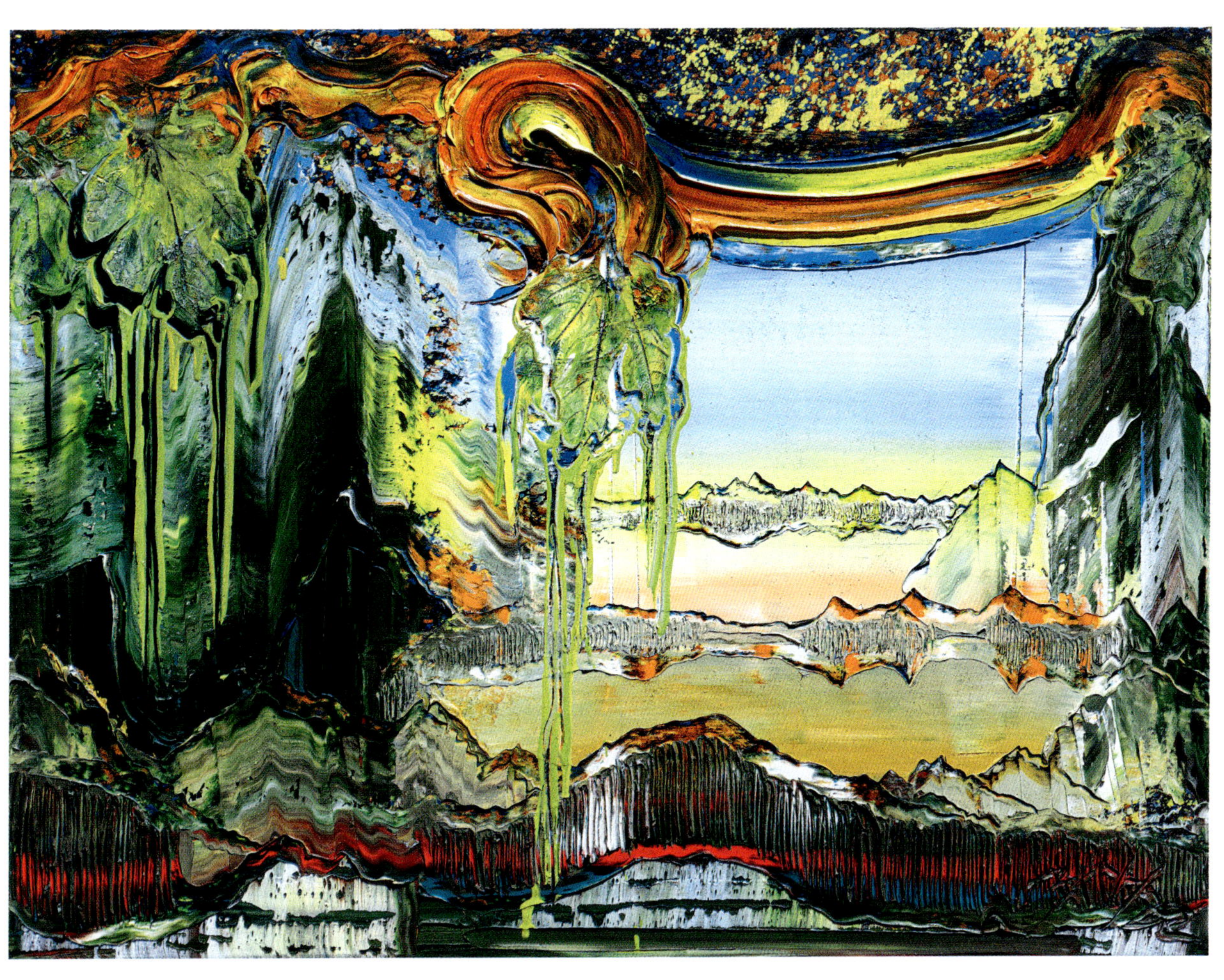

Journey
2022, 60 × 80 cm

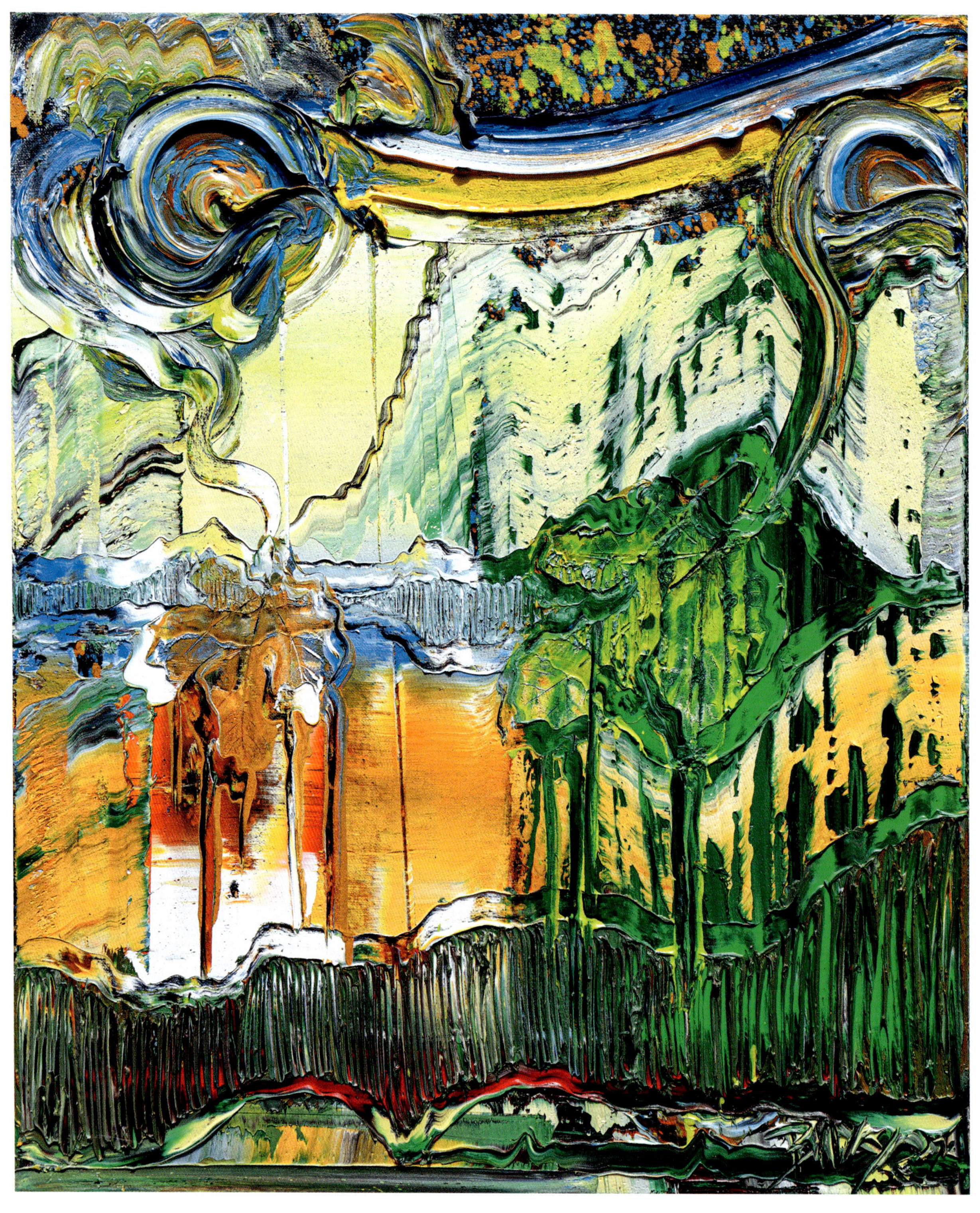

Journey
2022, 60 × 50 cm

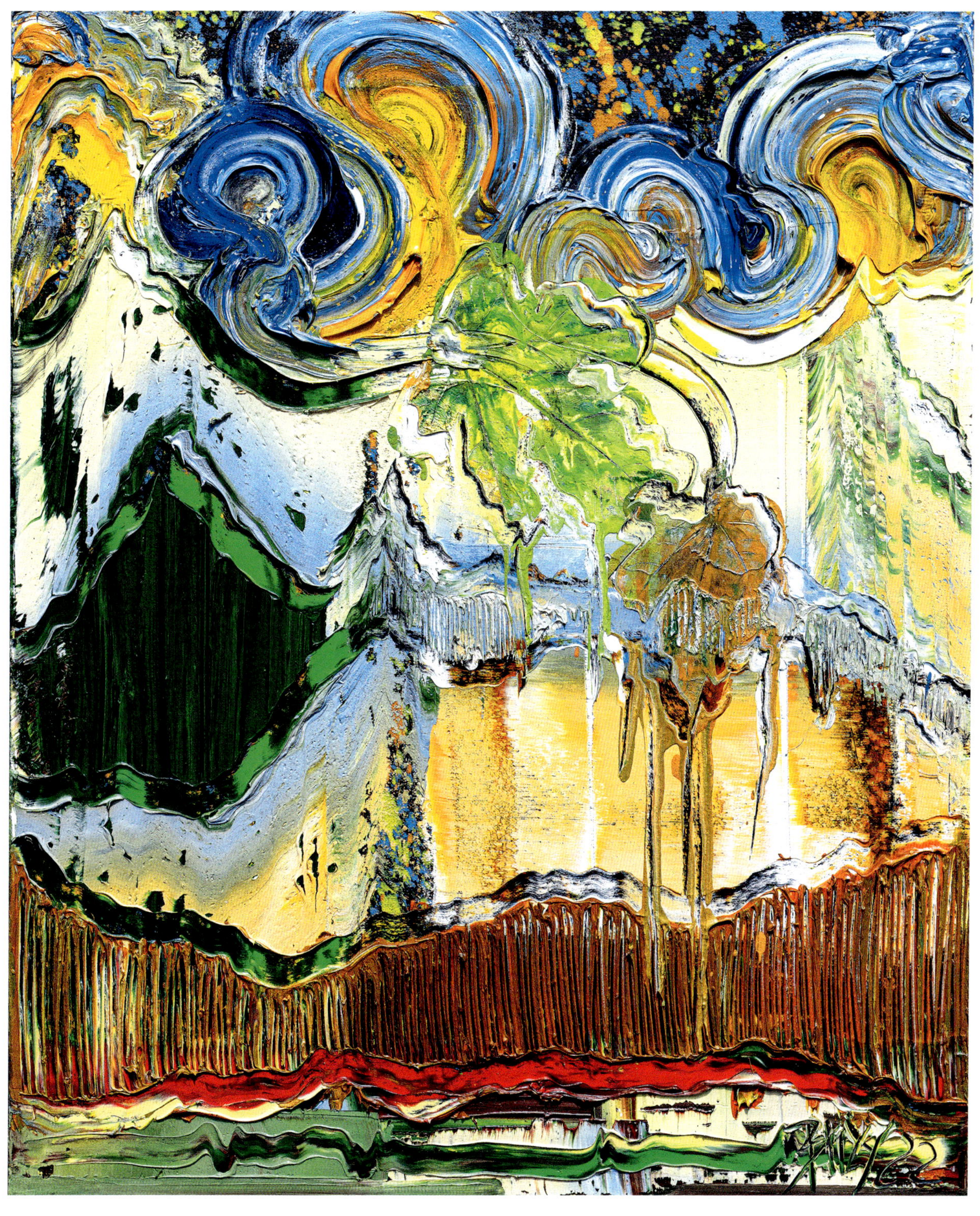

Journey
2022, 60 × 50 cm

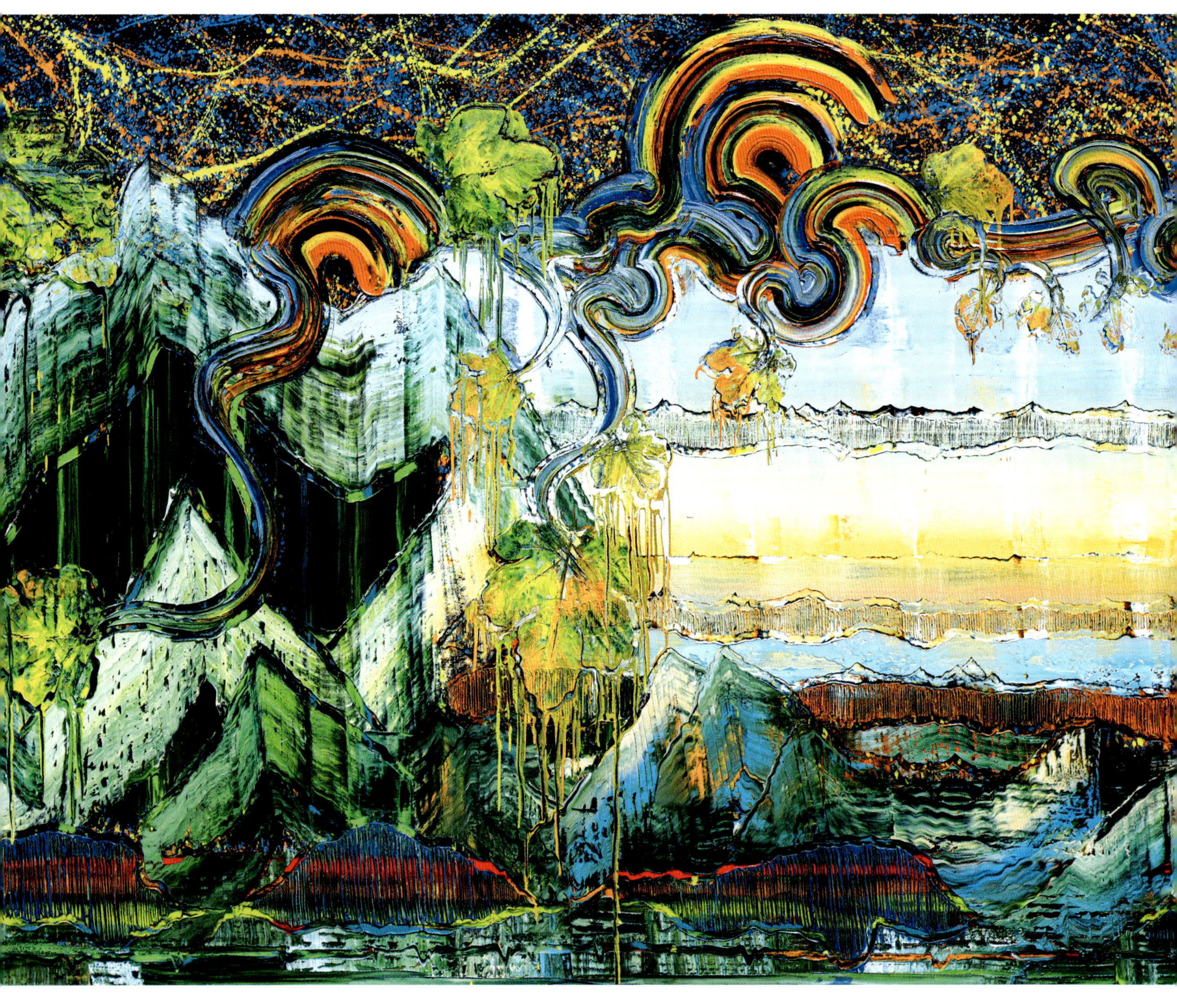

Journey
2022, 160 × 420 cm
Diptychon / diptych

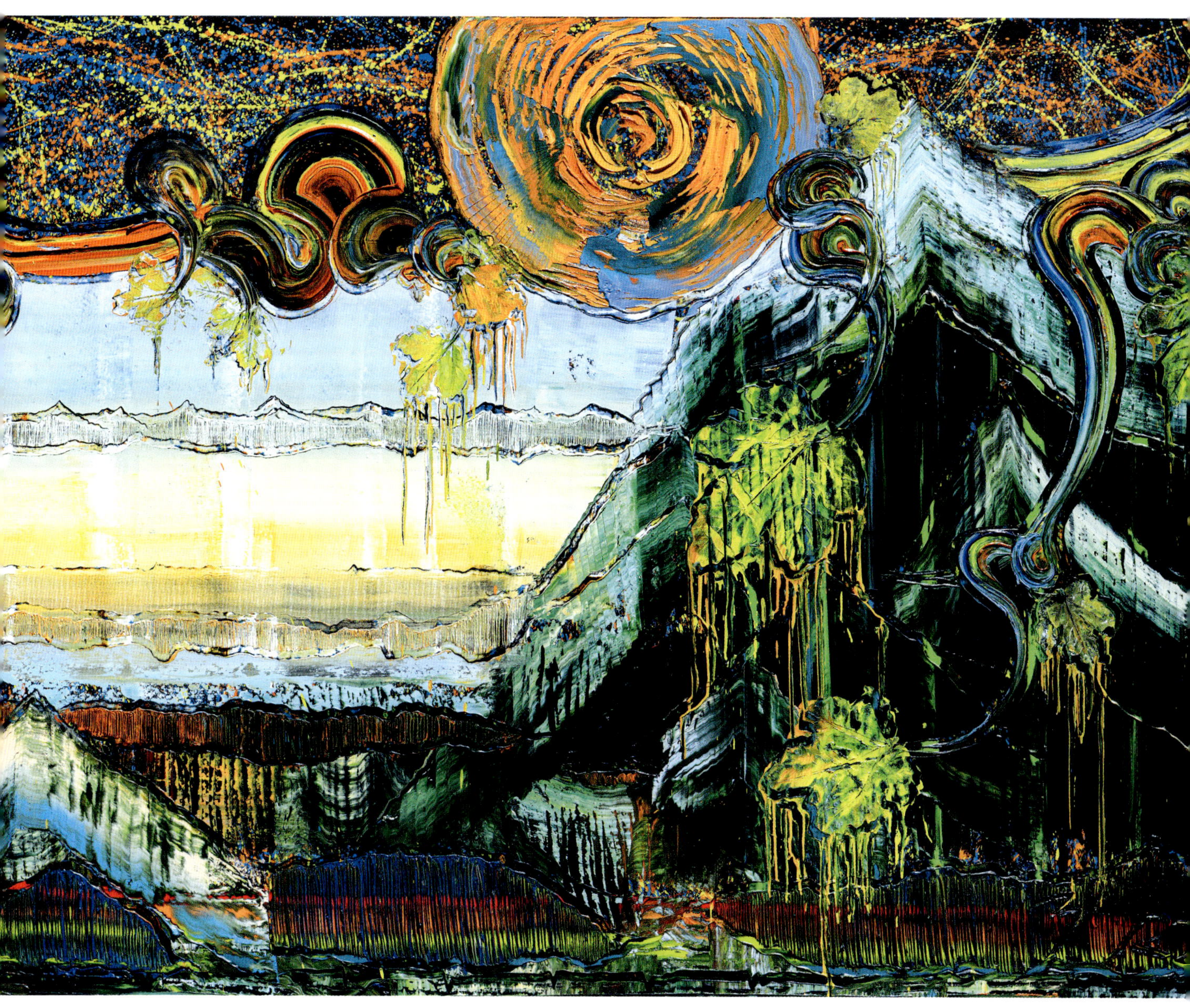

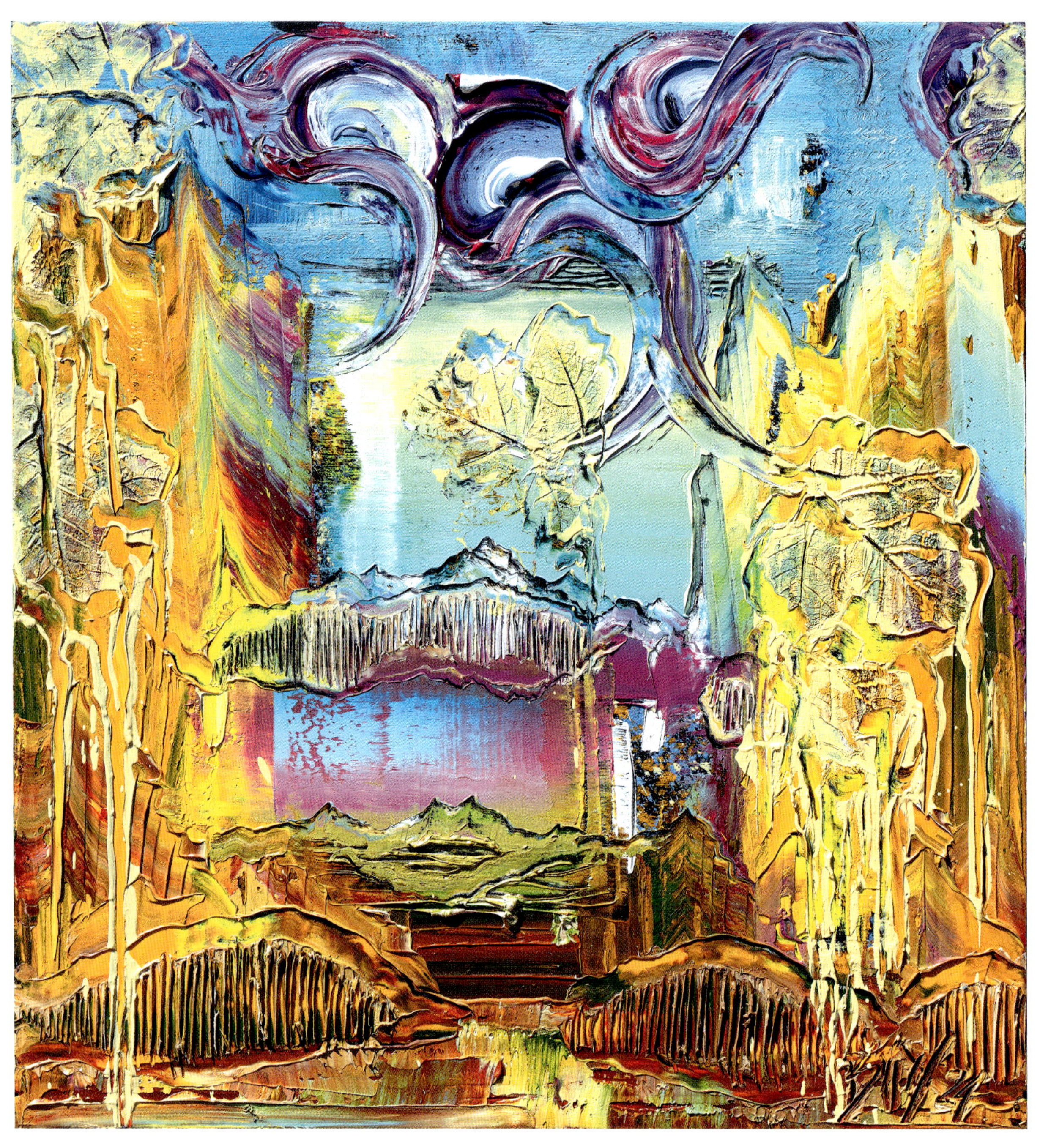

Journey
2024, 54 × 51 cm

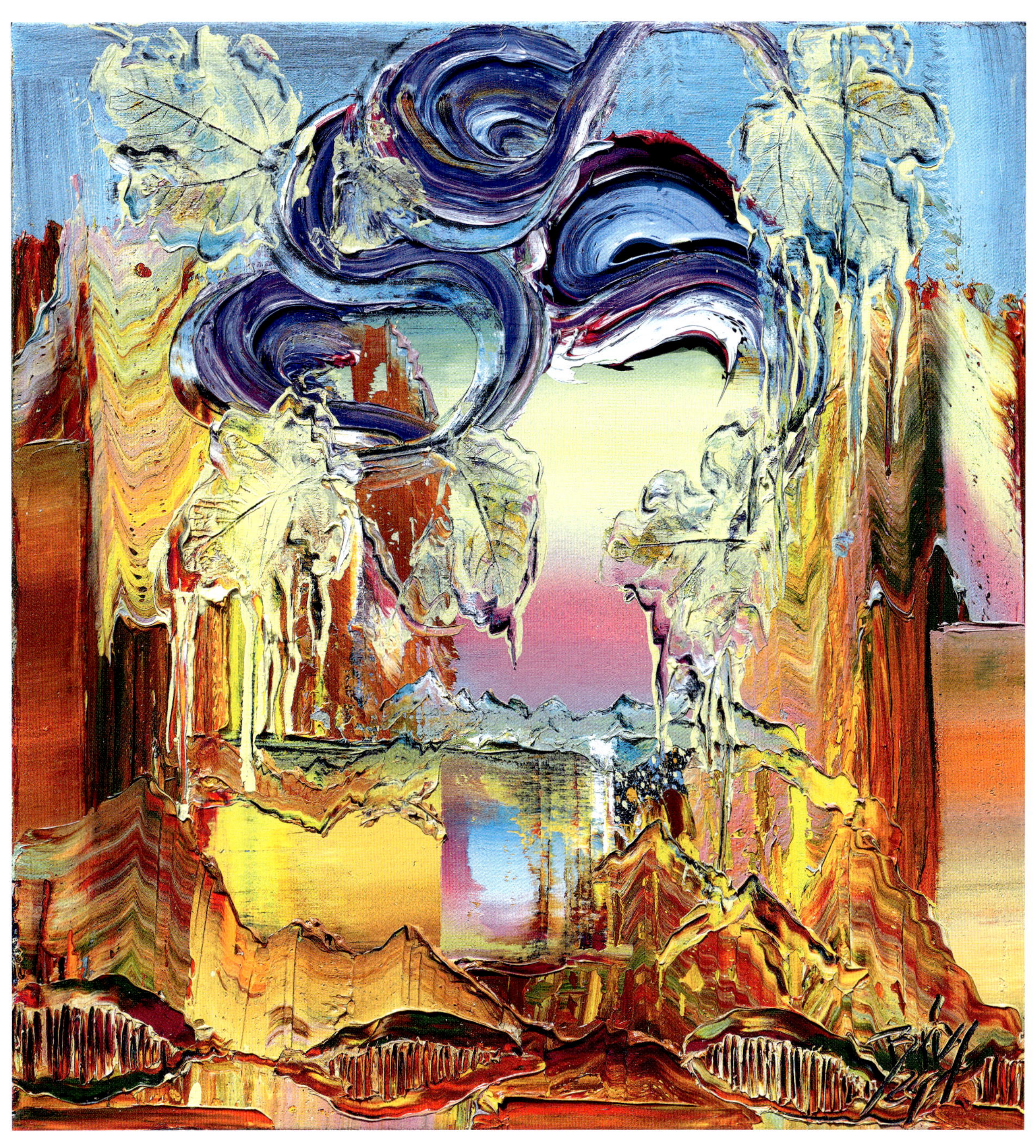

Journey
2024, 54 × 51 cm

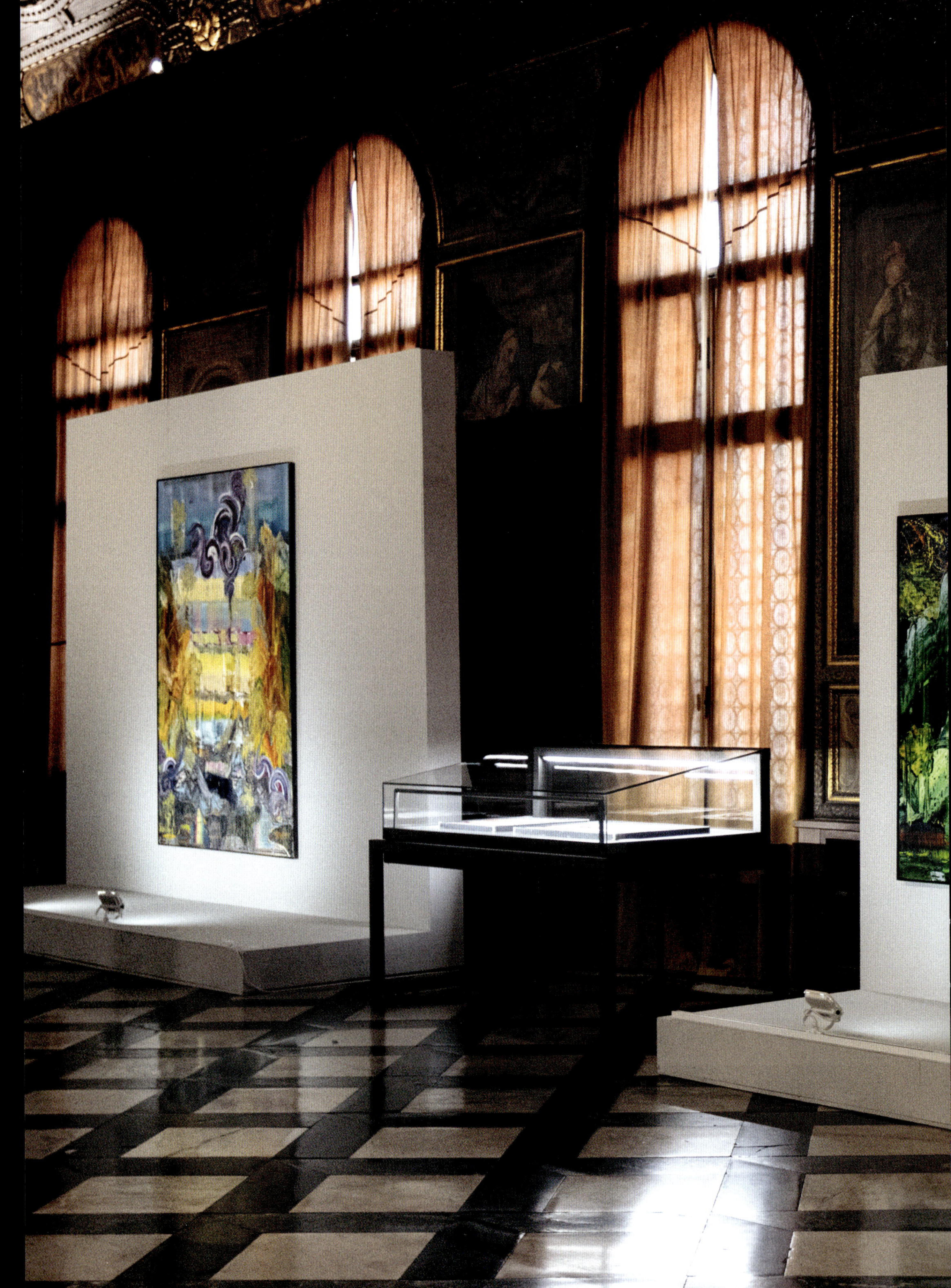

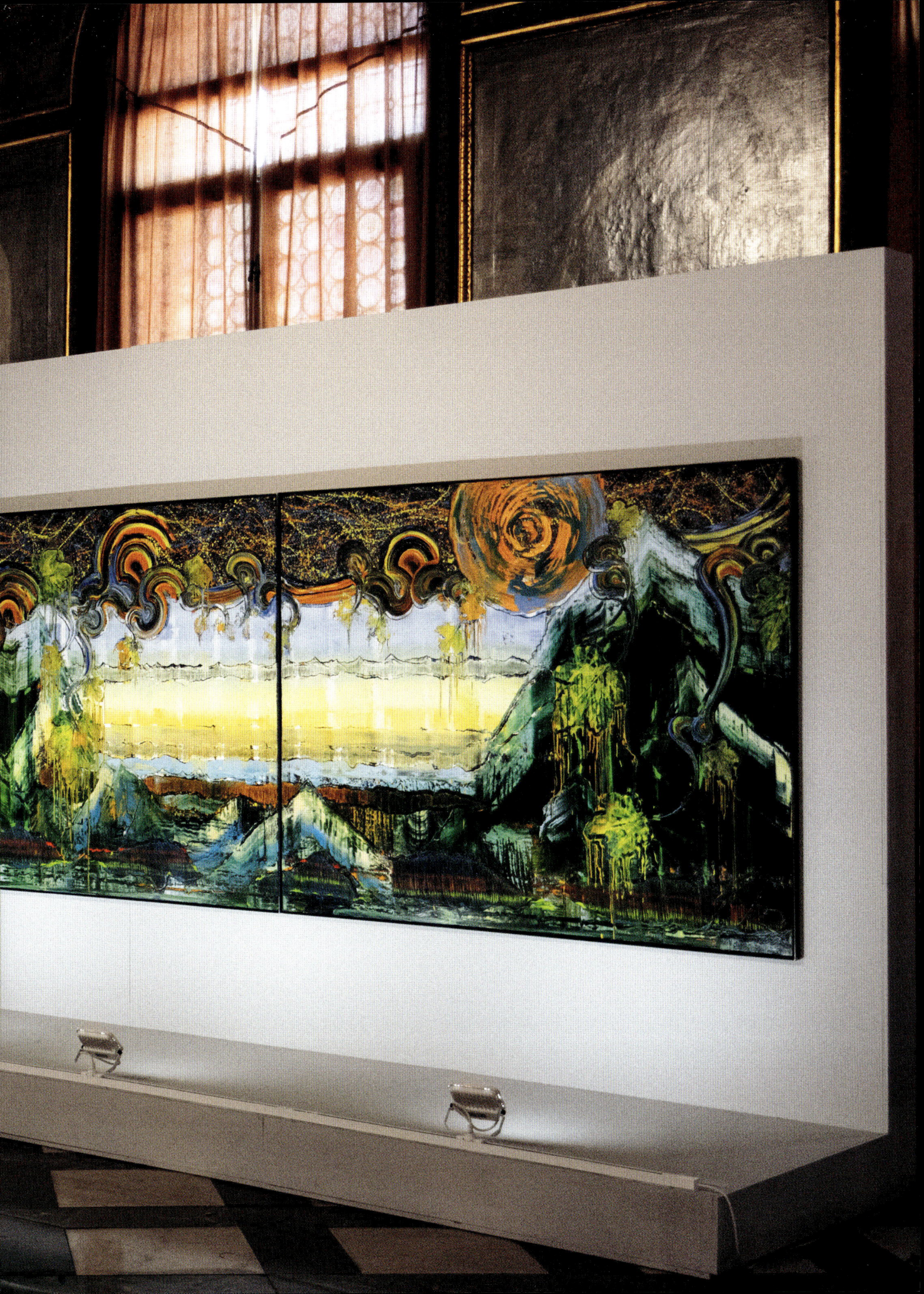

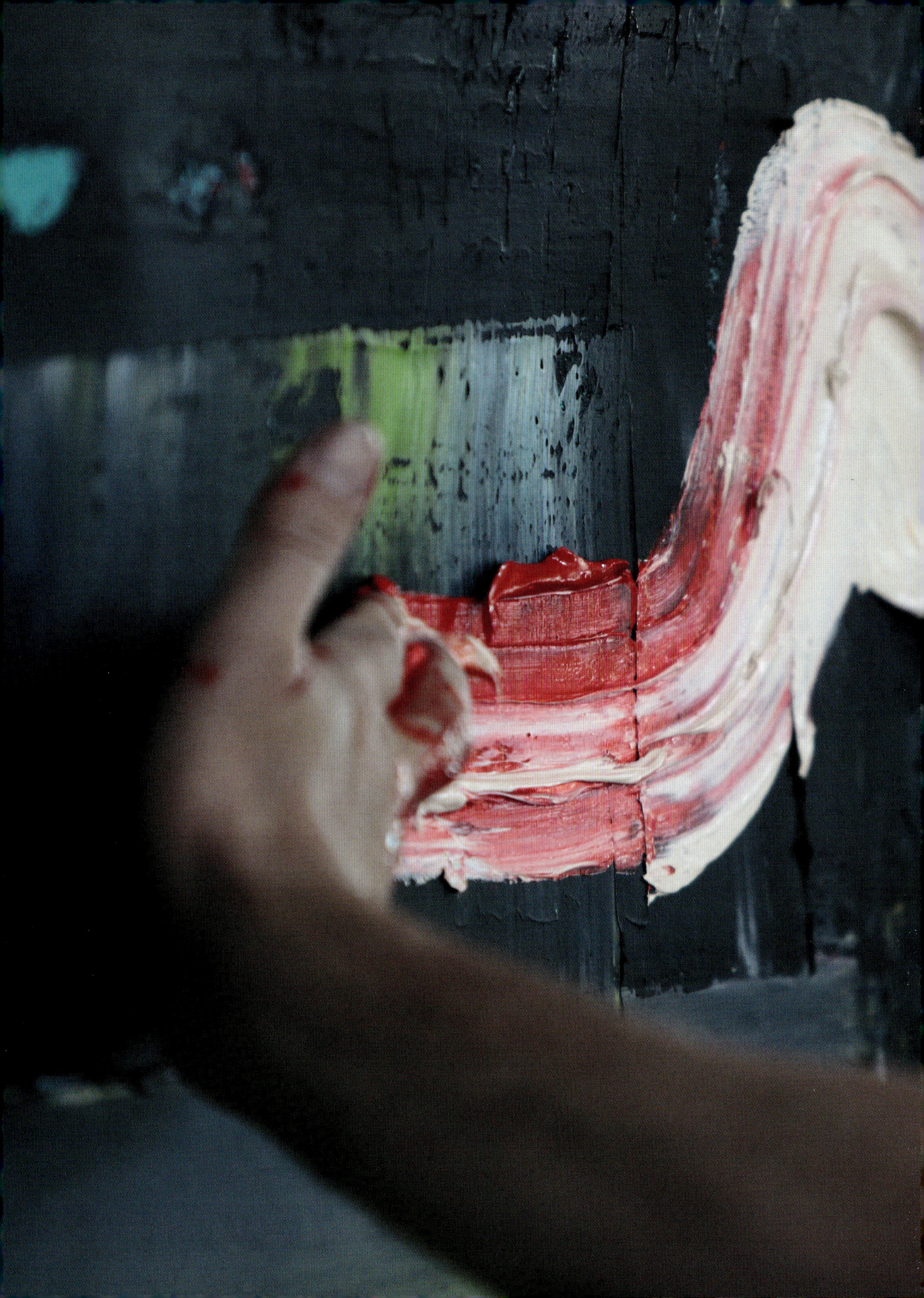

»DAS MALEN MIT DEN HÄNDEN VERBINDET MICH DIREKT MIT DER LEINWAND UND LÄSST MEINE GEDANKEN FREI FLIESSEN.«

»PAINTING WITH MY HANDS ESTABLISHES AN IMMEDIATE CONNECTION TO THE CANVAS, ENABLING MY THOUGHTS TO FLOW UNIMPEDED.«

Dietmar Brixy

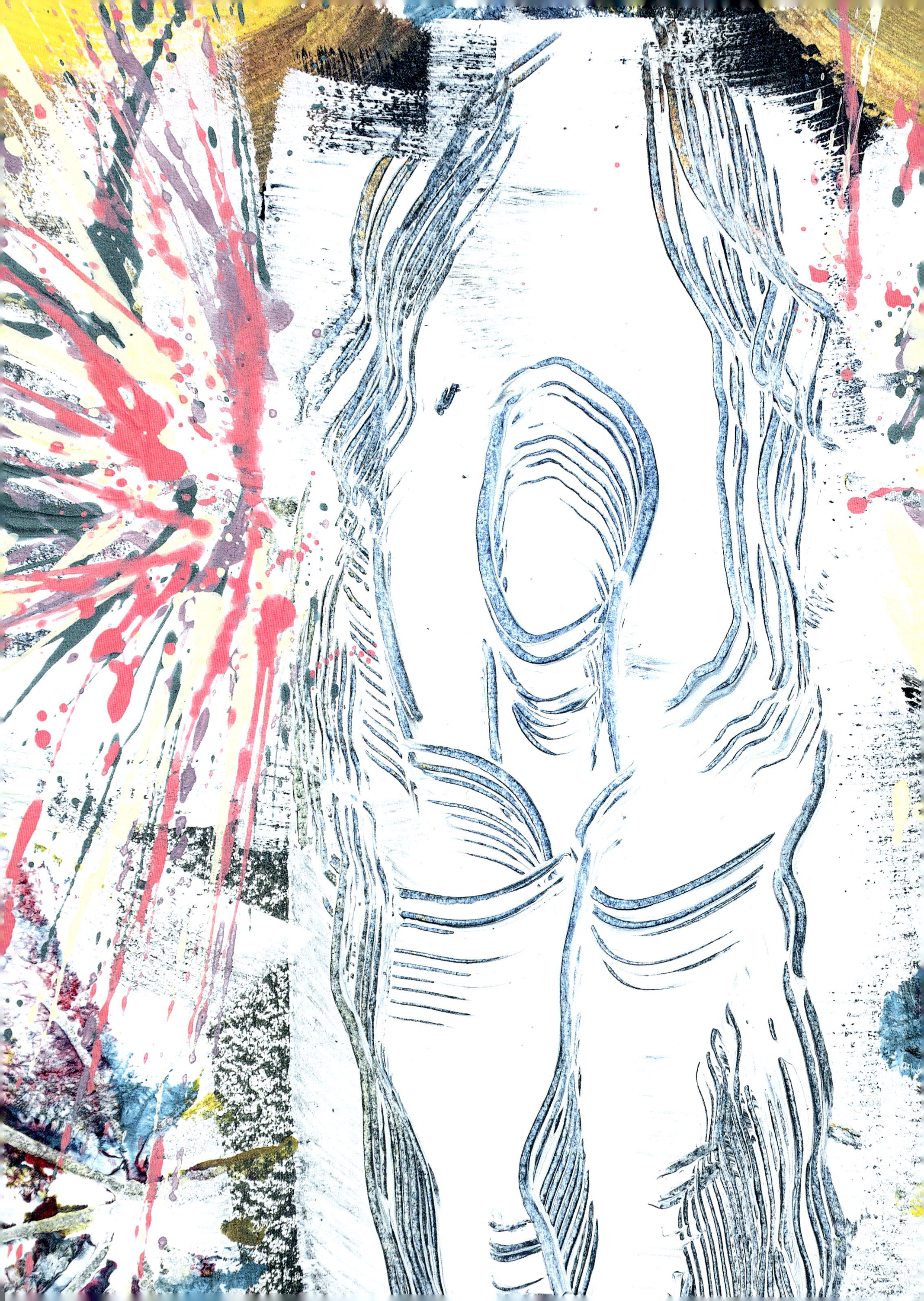

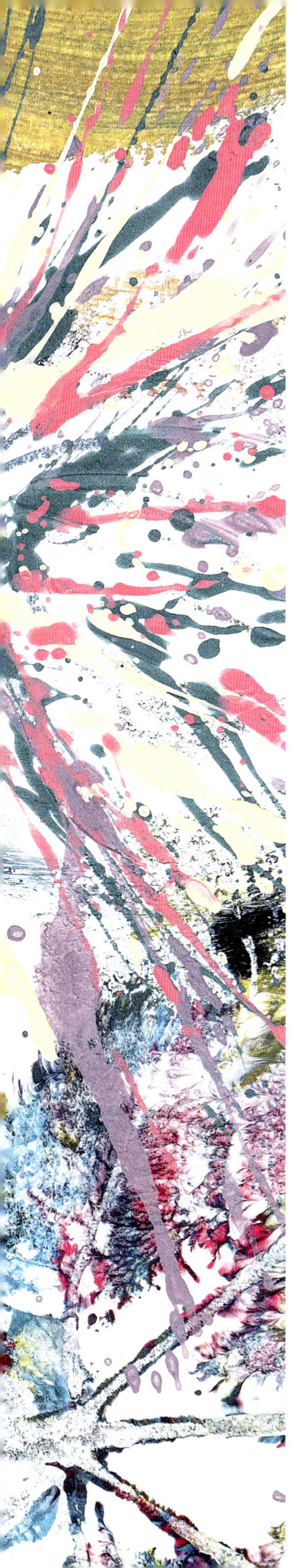

ARBEITEN AUF PAPIER

WORKS ON PAPER

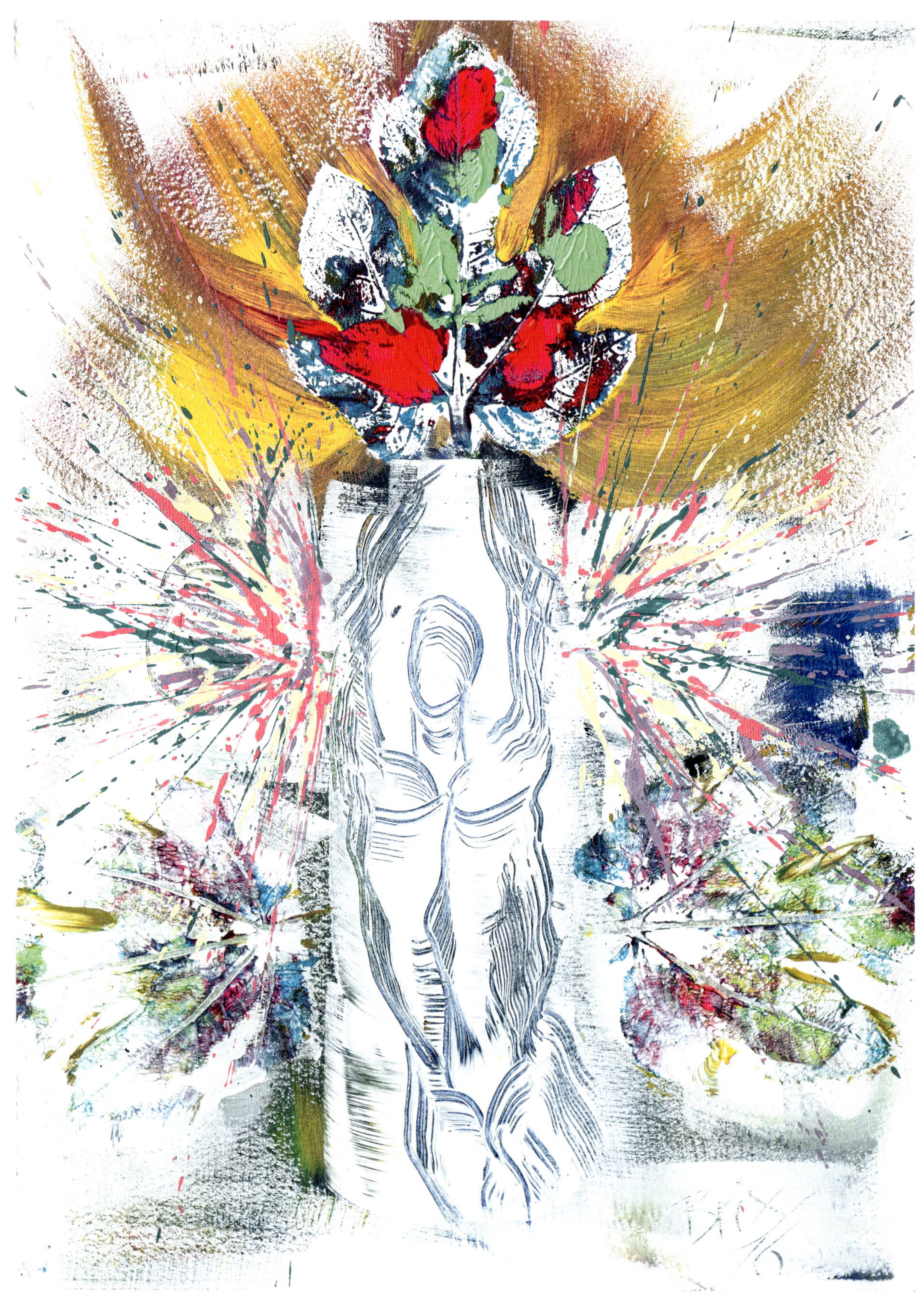

Eden
2016, 37 × 27 cm

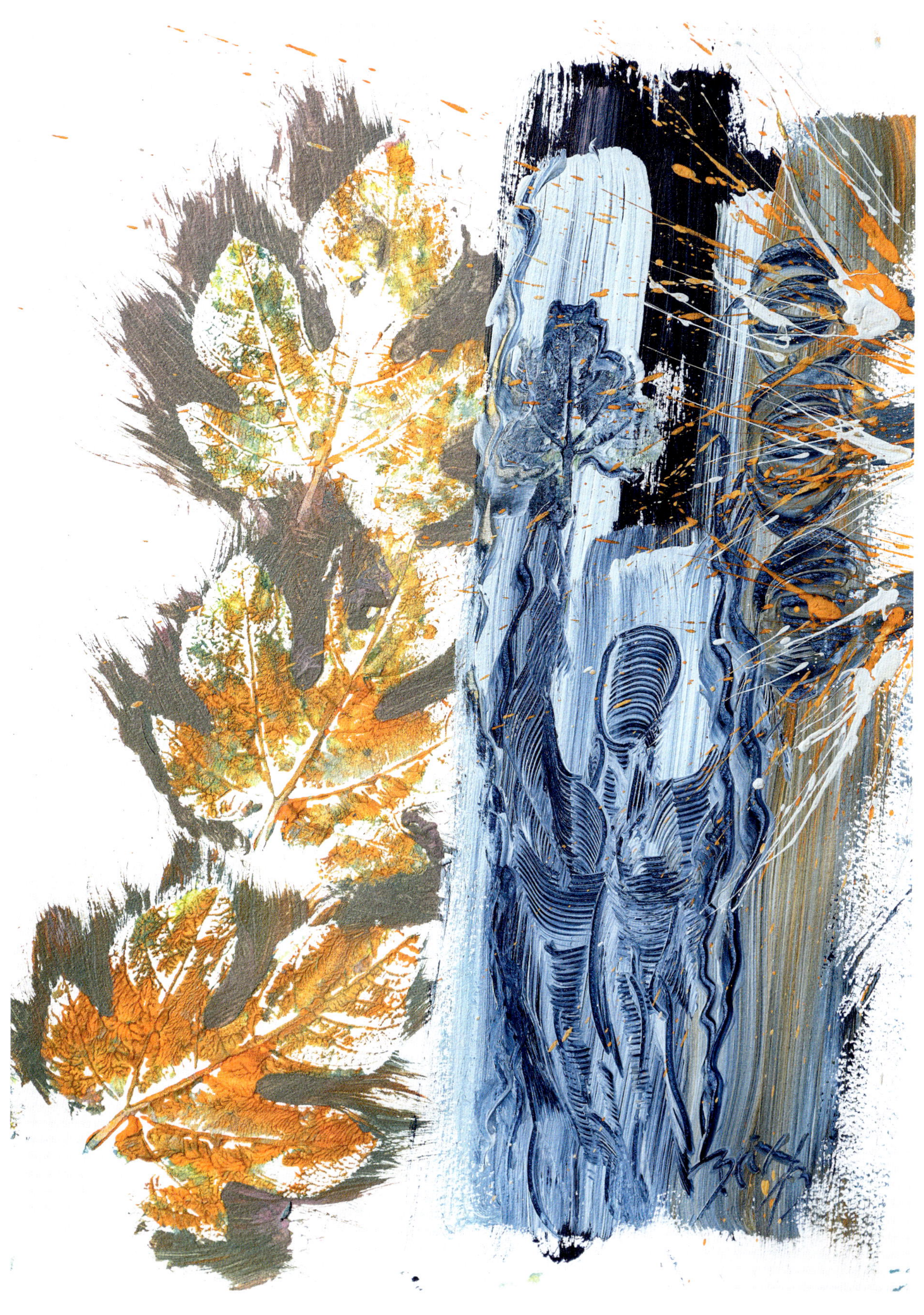

Eden
2013, 37 × 27 cm

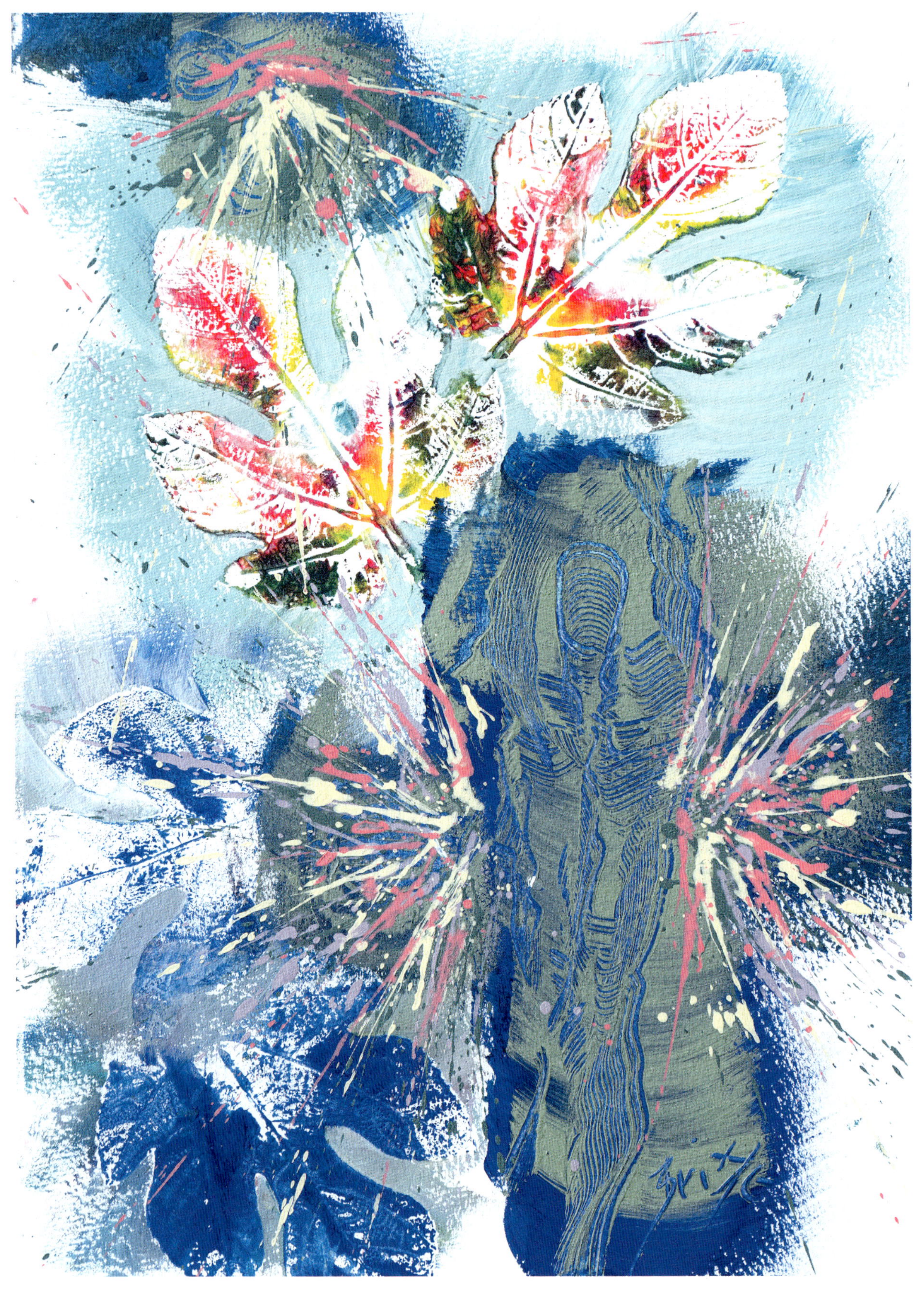

Eden
2016, 37 × 27 cm

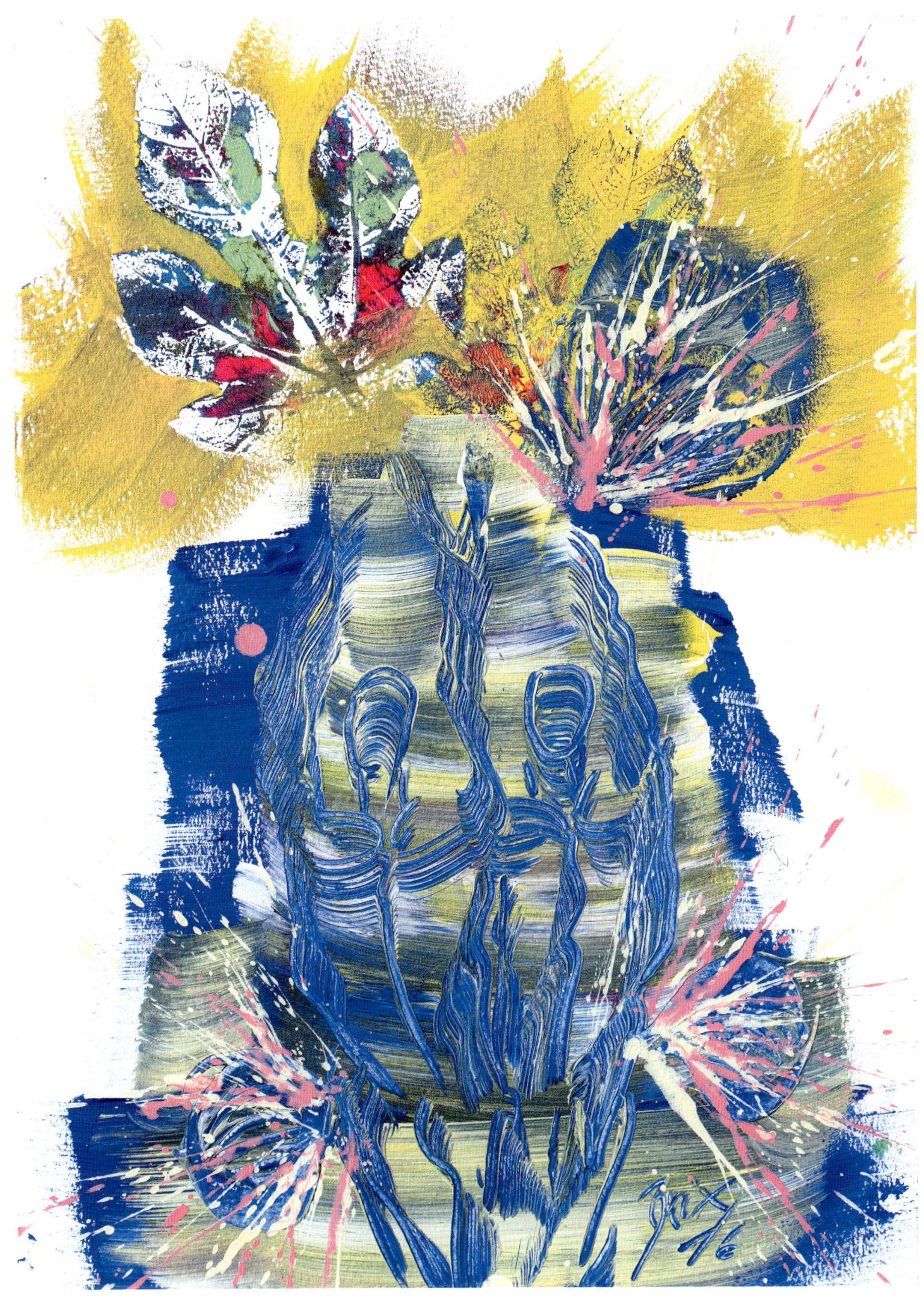

Eden
2016, 37 × 27 cm

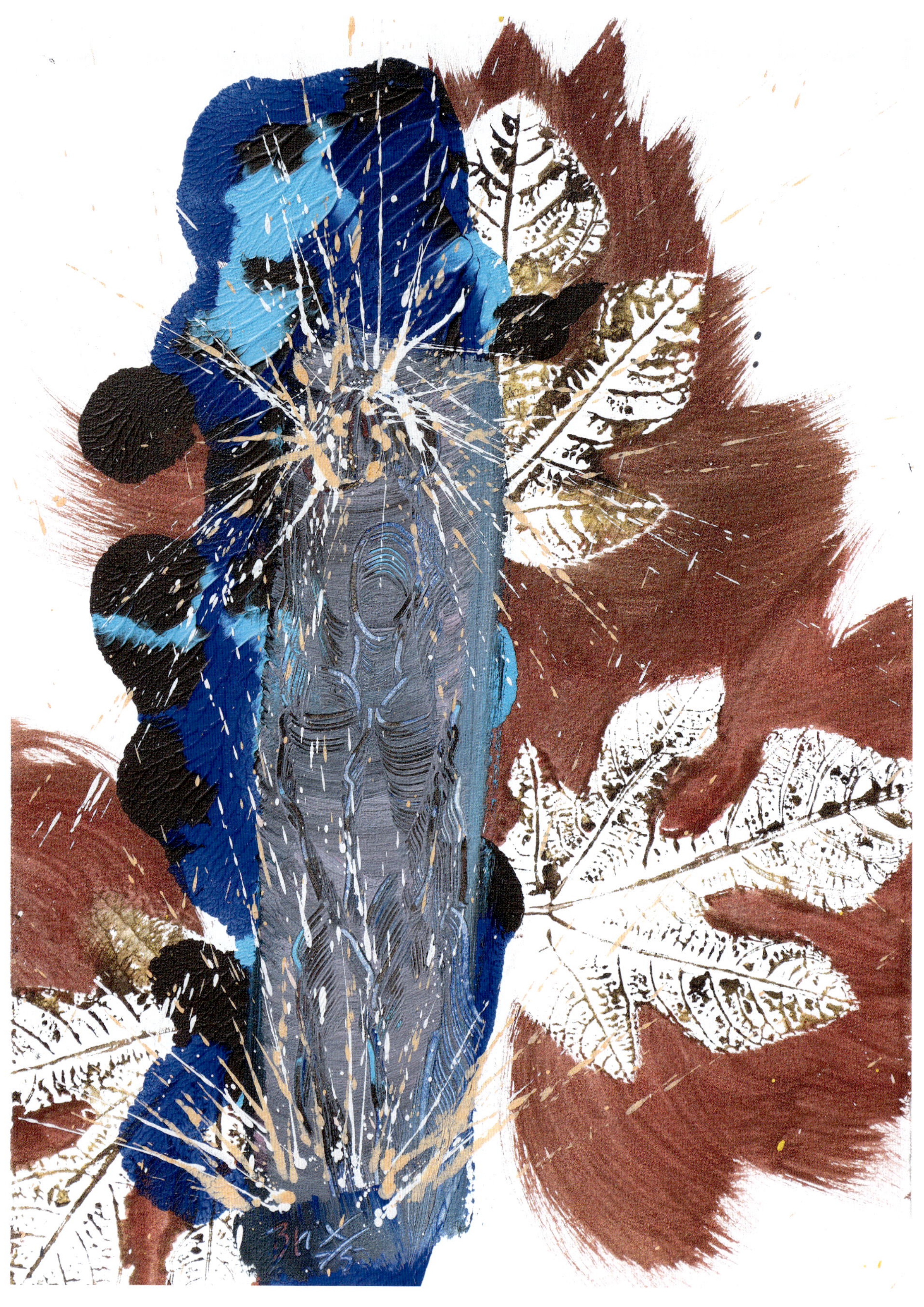

Eden
2015, 37 × 27 cm

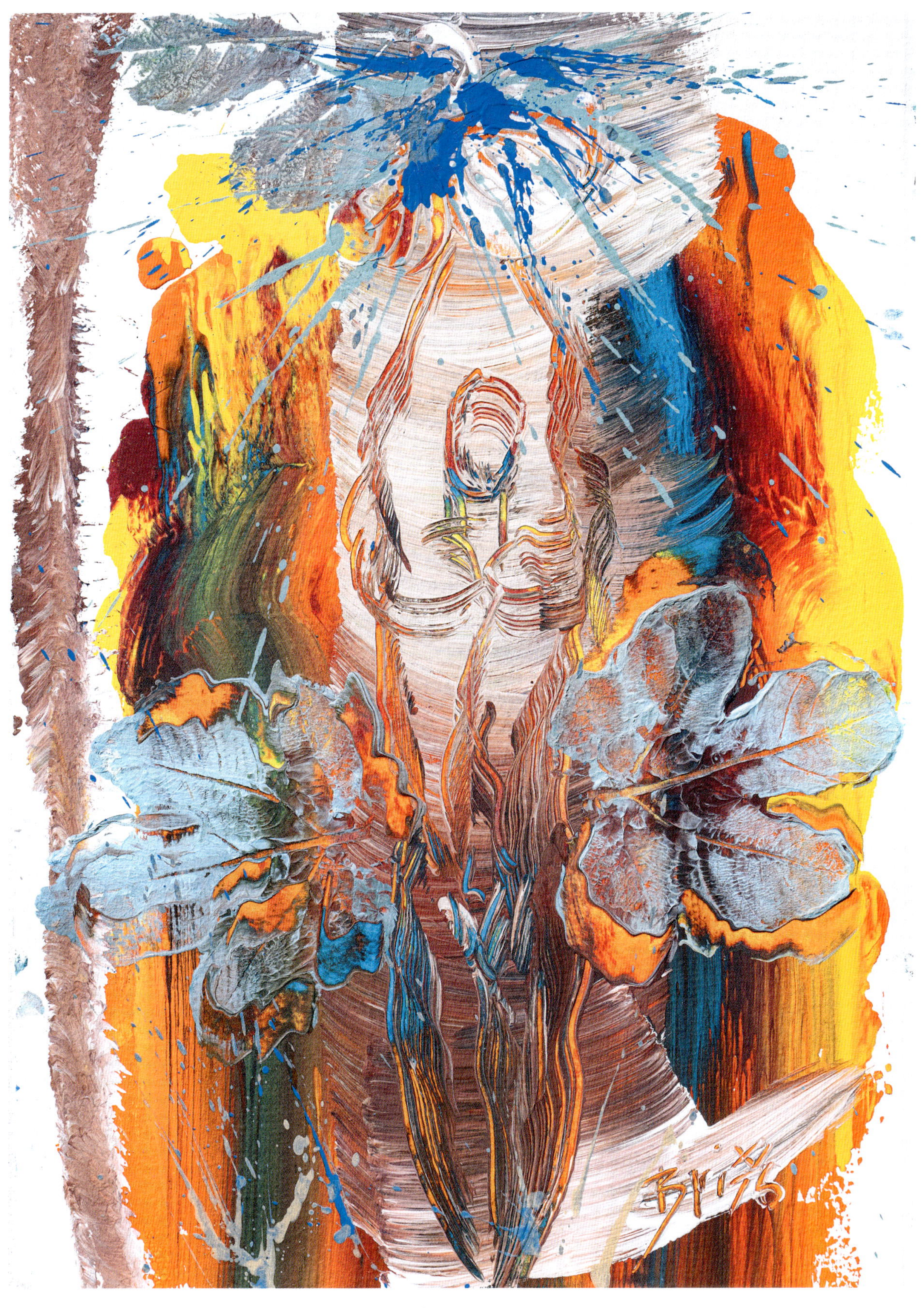

Eden
2016, 37 × 27 cm

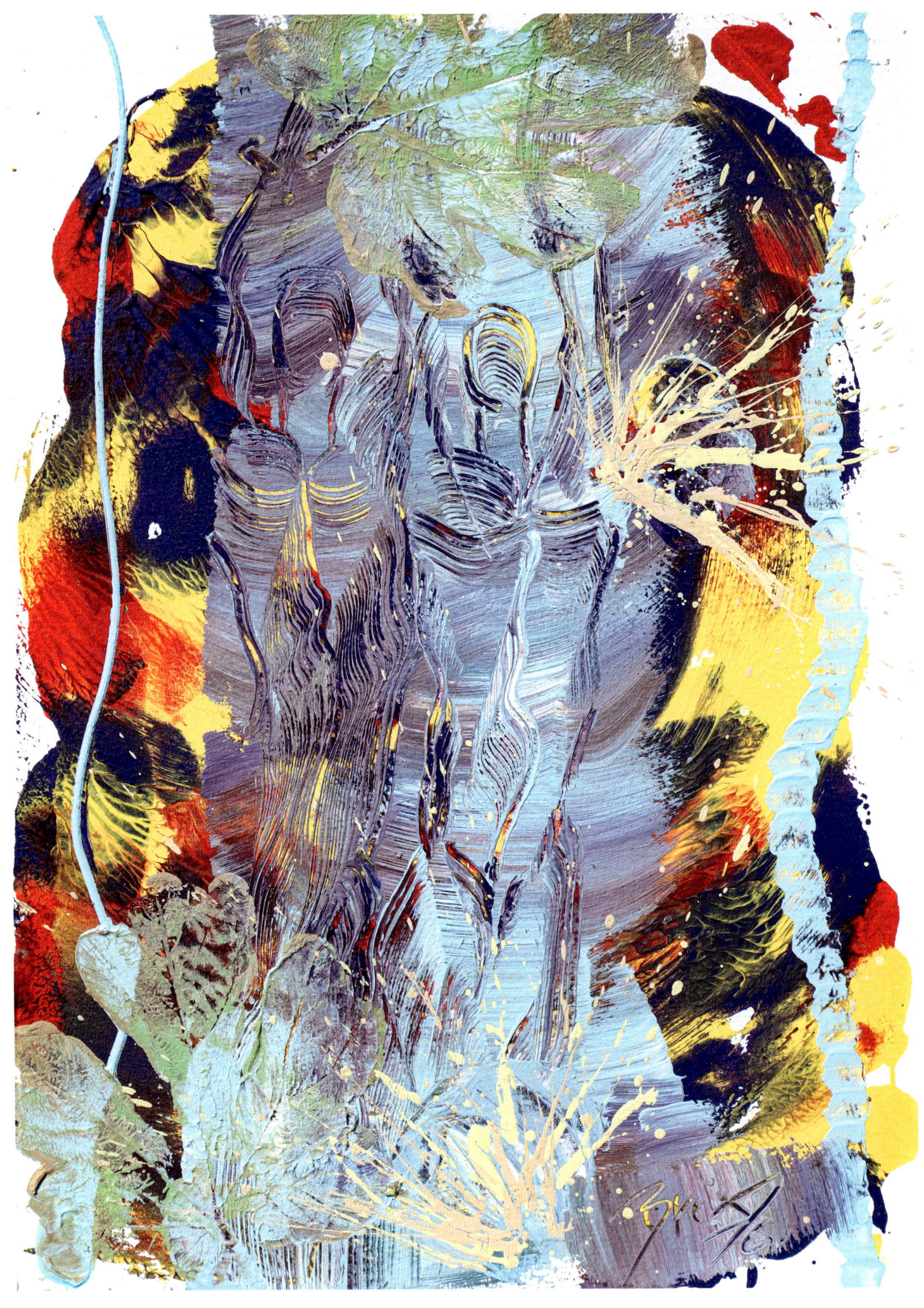

Eden
2016, 37 × 27 cm

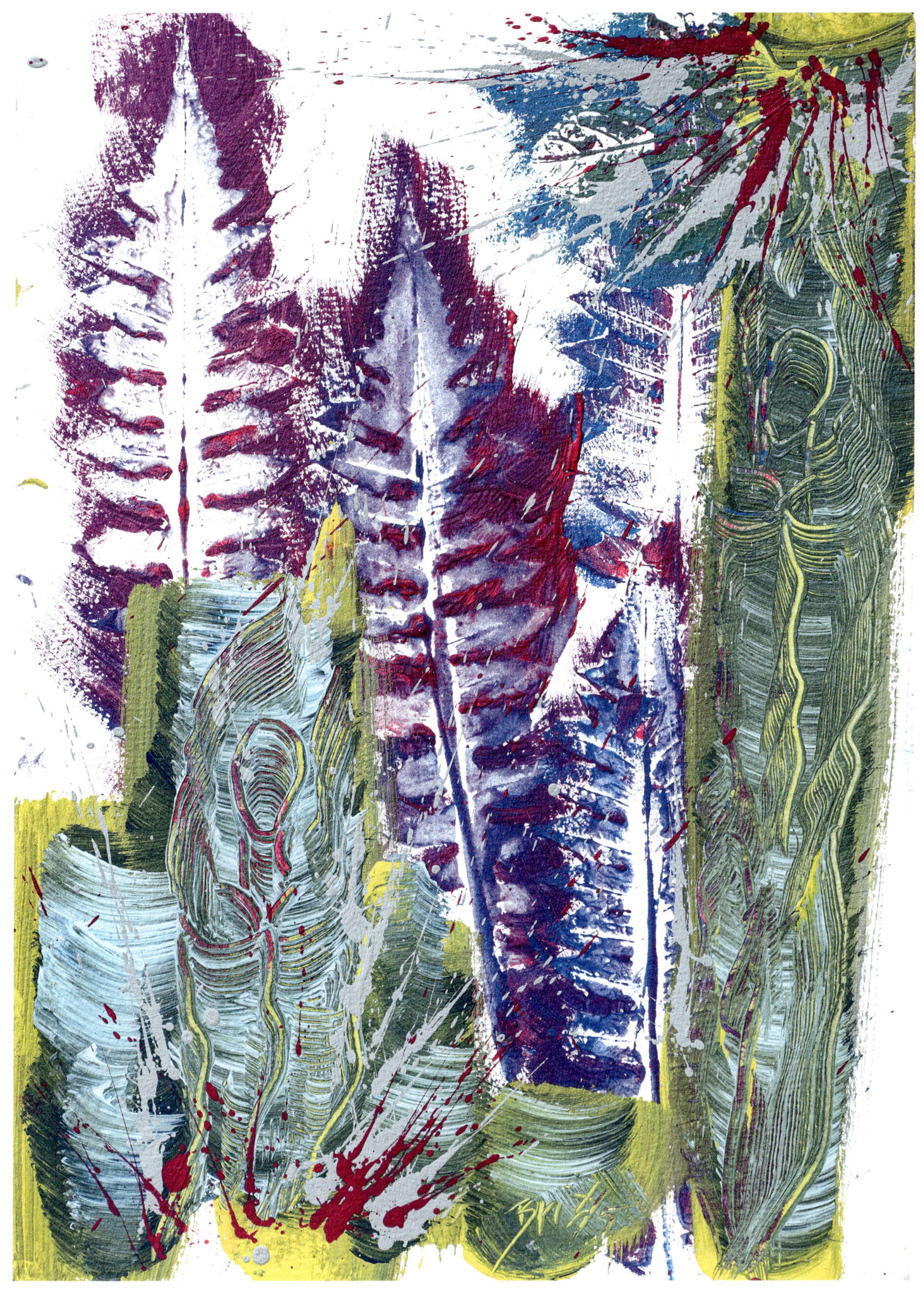

Eden
2015, 37 × 27 cm

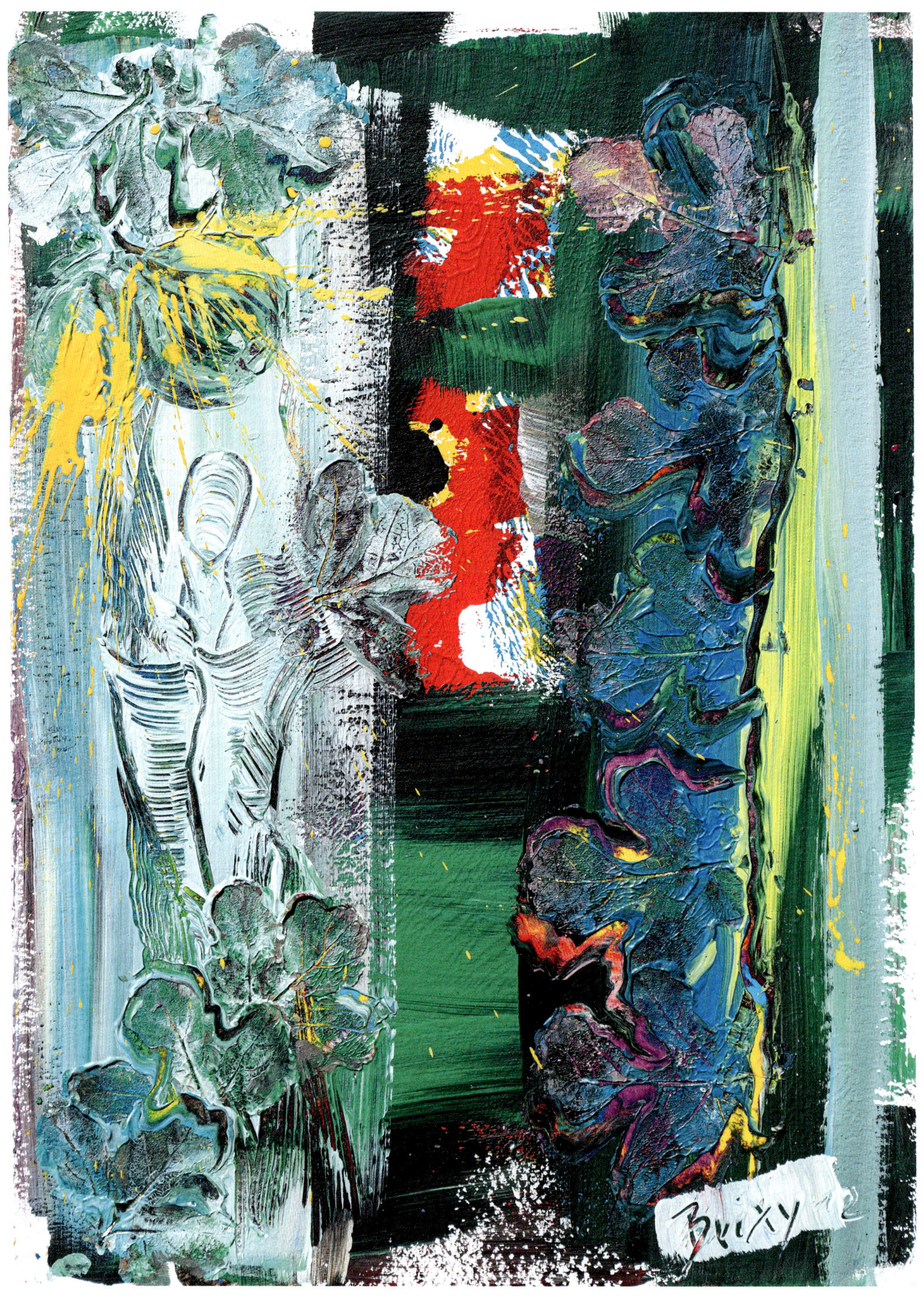

Eden
2012, 37 × 27 cm

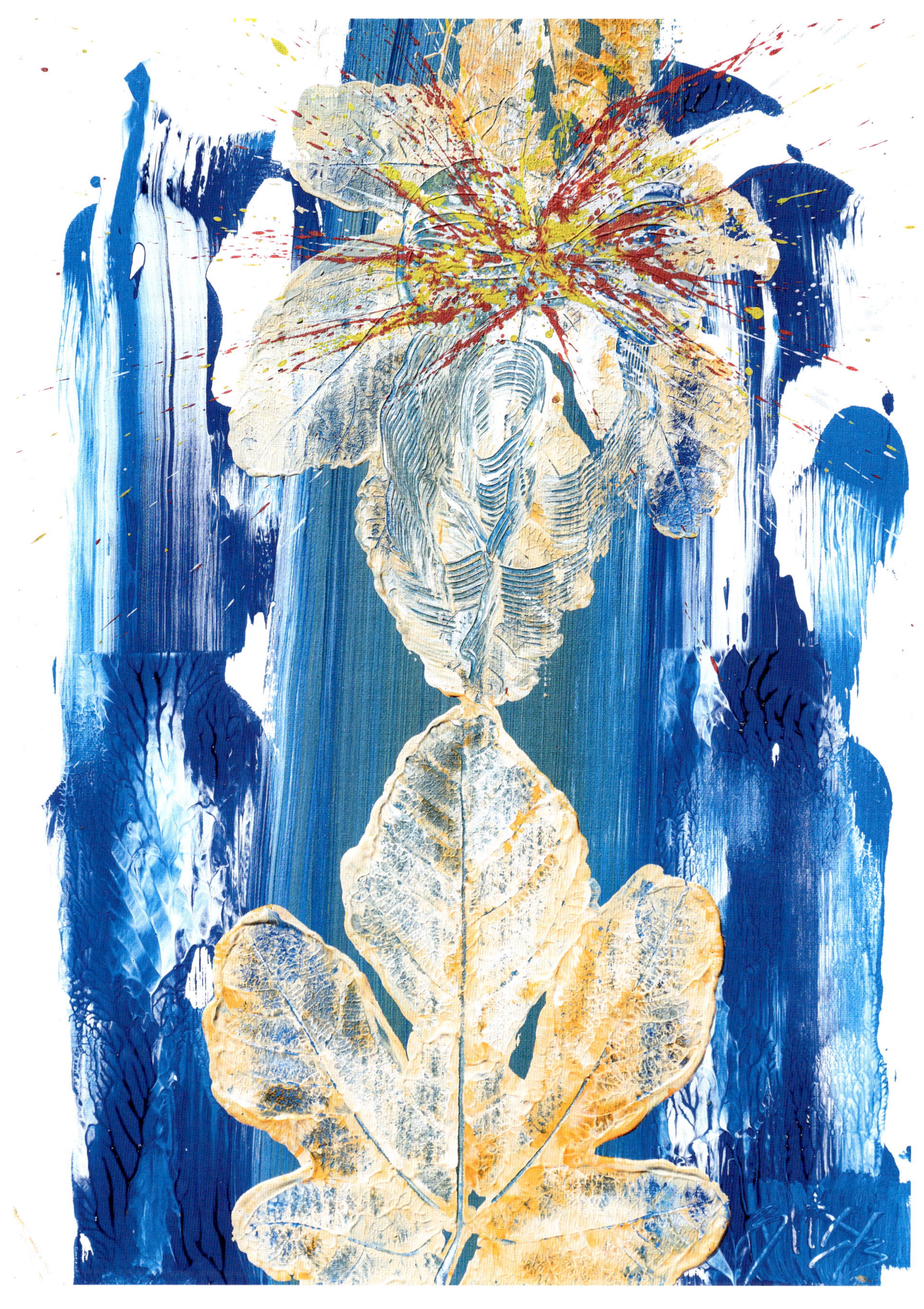

Eden
2013, 37 × 27 cm

EDITION:
IL MILIONE
DIE WUNDER DER WELT
THE WONDERS OF THE WORLD

Die Edition erscheint anlässlich der Ausstellung *Brixy – The Description of the World* in der Biblioteca Nazionale Marciana, Venedig, parallel zur Biennale Arte 2024.

Originalwerk: Journey, 2024, Öl auf Nessel, 80 × 60 cm
Format: 80 × 60 cm (gerahmt)
Technik: Pigmentdruck auf Büttenpapier mit gerissenen Kanten im weißen Rahmen auf weißem Passepartout
Kennzeichnung: Jedes Exemplar ist handsigniert, nummeriert und individuell durch den Künstler von Hand überarbeitet.
Jahr: 2024
Auflage: 35 Exemplare

The edition is published on the occasion of the exhibition *Brixy – The Description of the World* at the Biblioteca Nazionale Marciana, Venice, in parallel to the Biennale Arte 2024.

Original work: Journey, 2024, oil on nettle, 80 × 60 cm
Format: 80 × 60 cm sheet in frame
Technique: Pigment print on laid paper with torn edges in a white frame on a white passe-partout
Labeling: Each copy is signed, numbered and individually reworked by hand by the artist
Year: 2024
Edition: 35 copies

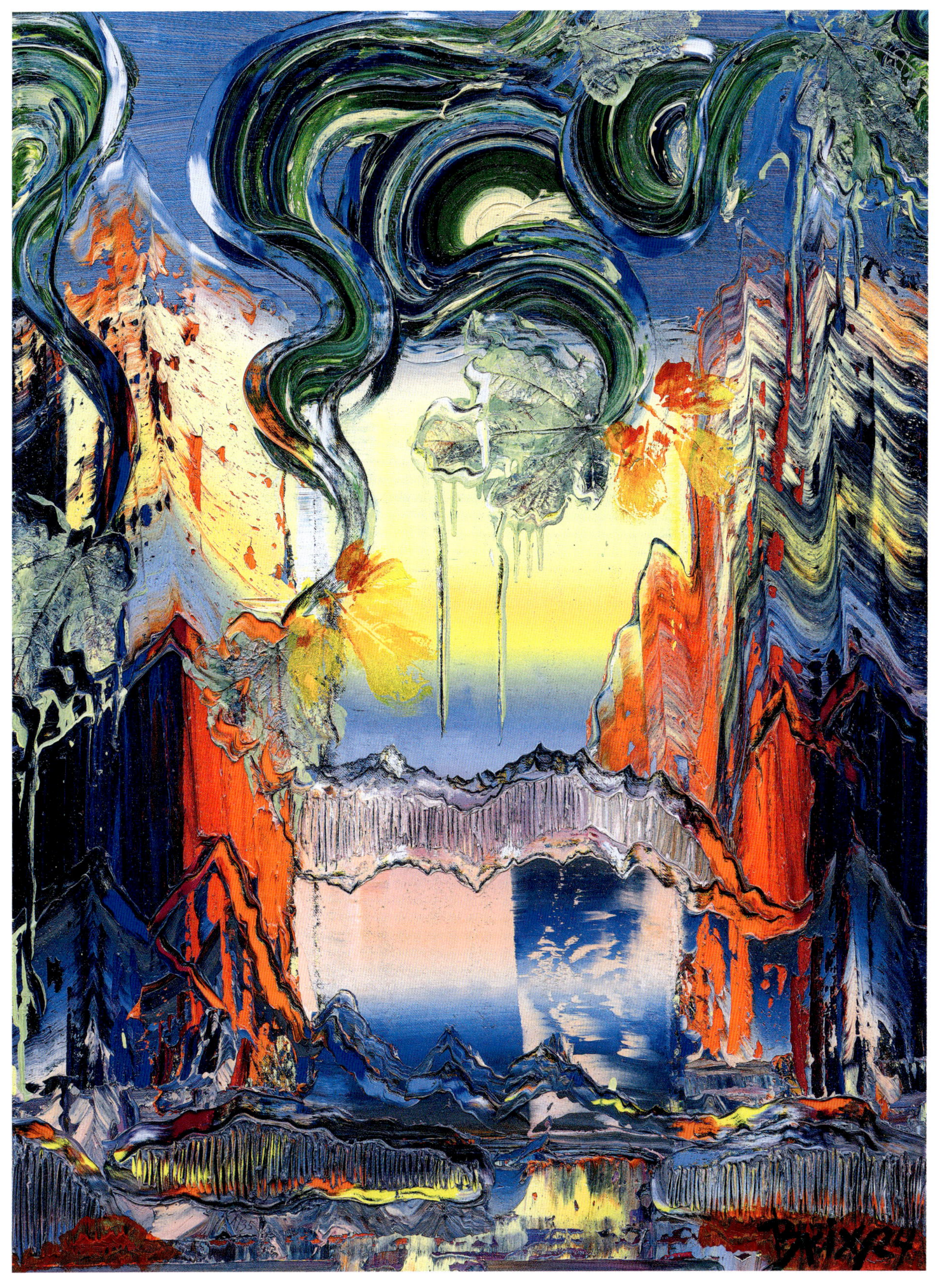

Il Milione
2024, 80 × 60 cm
Ex. 1/35

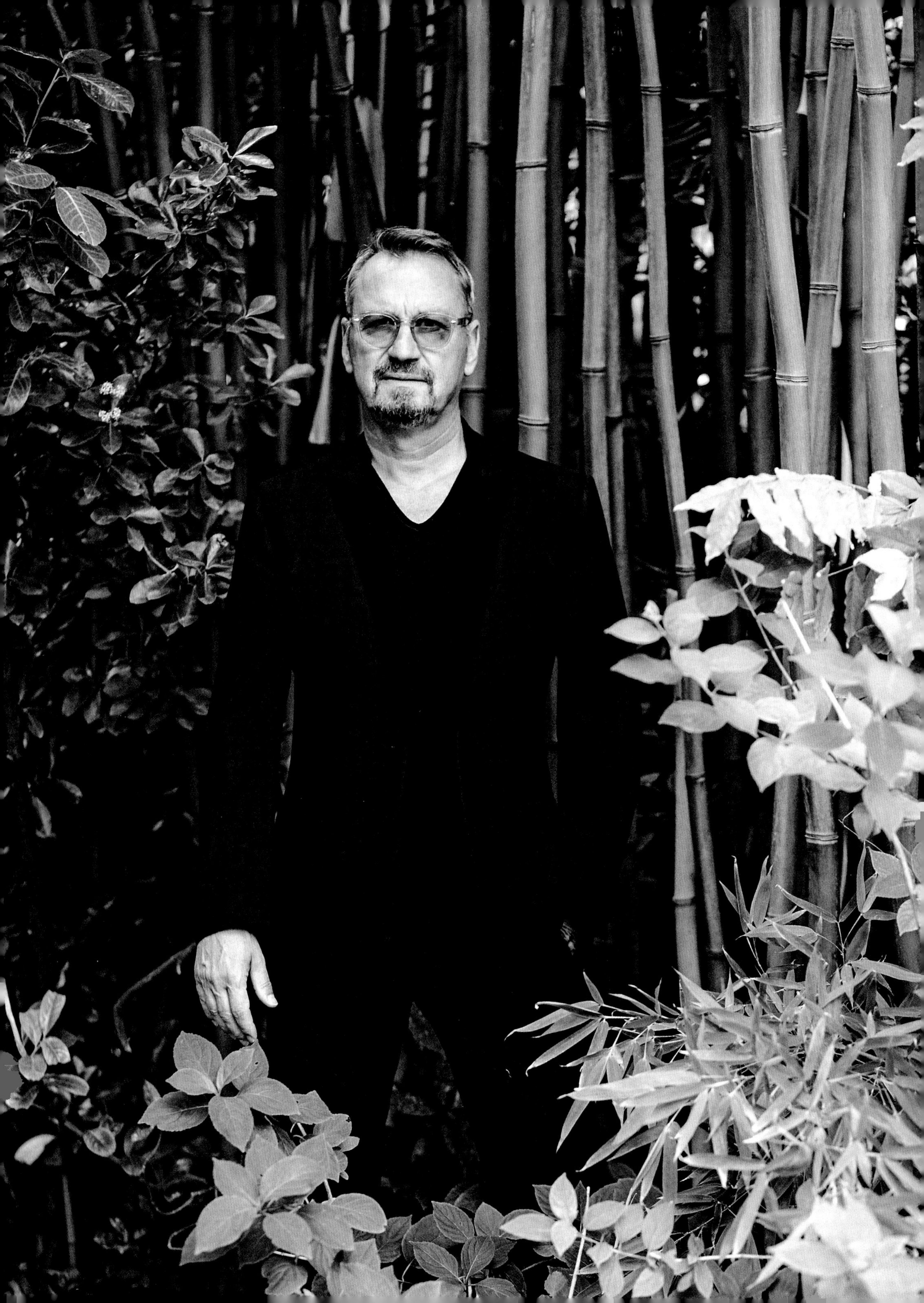

BIOGRAFIE / BIOGRAPHY

Dietmar Brixy wurde 1961 in Mannheim geboren. Er studierte von 1985 bis 1991 an der Staatlichen Akademie der Bildenden Künste in Karlsruhe, unter anderem bei den Professoren Wilhelm Loth, Katharina Fritsch und Harald Klingelhöller. Seit 1991 lebt und arbeitet er als freischaffender Künstler in Mannheim, wo er im Jahr 2001 das neugotische Alte Pumpwerk erwarb und das ehemalige Industriegebäude denkmalgerecht zu seinem Wohn- und Atelierhaus mit einer kunstvoll gestalteten Gartenlandschaft umbaute. Hierfür erhielt er mehrere Preise, unter anderem von der Denkmalstiftung Baden-Württemberg.

Die Natur dient Brixy als wichtigste Inspirationsquelle für seine Kunst. Seine Malereien sprechen eine eigene, expressiv-lebendige Sprache, die er seinen Kompositionen mit Pinseln, Spachteln, Kämmen und anderen Werkzeugen einhaucht. Er wird buchstäblich „handgreiflich" und formt die pastosen Ölfarben wie ein Bildhauer direkt mit seinen Händen, um ihnen organische und vegetabile Strukturen zu verleihen. Brixy bewegt sich zwischen abstraktem Action Painting und figurativer Geste. Er entwickelte eine unverkennbare Art, mehrere Farbschichten zu vibrierenden Bildern zu modellieren.

Dietmar Brixy is a German painter and sculptor. He was born in Mannheim in 1961 and studied at the State Academy of Fine Arts in Karlsruhe from 1985 to 1991, where his teachers included professors Wilhelm Loth, Katharina Fritsch, and Harald Klingelhöller. He has been living and working as a full time artist in Mannheim since 1991. In 2001, he purchased the NeoGothic Altes Pumpwerk (a disused pumping station) in the Neckarau district of Mannheim and has since lovingly restored the old industrial building, converting it into a living space and studio surrounded by gardens. He has won several awards for the renovation, for example, from the historical monument society of the Denkmalstiftung Baden-Württemberg.

Nature is the primary source of inspiration for Brixy's art. His paintings speak a distinctive, expressive, and animated language that the artist weaves into his compositions through his vigorous use of brushes, palette knives, combs, and other tools. The artist not only uses tools to create his paintings but is quite literally "hands on," shaping the thick impasto oils into organic and vegetal structures directly with his hands like a sculptor. Brixy has for years combined elements of abstract action painting and gestural figuration. The modeling of several layers of paint into vibrating images has long been his instantly recognizable signature style.

EINZELAUSSTELLUNGEN (AUSWAHL)
SOLO EXHIBITIONS (SELECTION)
2010–2024

2024
- Biblioteca Nazionale Marciana, Venedig / Venice
- Galerie Tammen, Berlin

2023
- art KARLSRUHE

2022
- Kunstverein Villa Streccius, Landau
- Galerie der Volksbank Kurpfalz eG, Weinheim

2021
- Galerie Tammen, Berlin
- Christian Marx Galerie, Düsseldorf

2020
- Galerie Barbara von Stechow, Frankfurt am Main
- art KARLSRUHE

2019
- MS Europa 2, Hamburg
- Kunsträume Zermatt, Schweiz / Switzerland
- CultureInside Gallery, Luxemburg / Luxembourg, unter Schirmherrschaft der Botschaft der BRD / under the auspices of the Embassy of the FRG

2018
- Christian Marx Galerie, Düsseldorf
- Galerie am Dom, Wetzlar

2017
- Europäisches Parlament, Brüssel, Belgien / European Parliament, Brussels, Belgium
- Galerie Cornelia Kamp, Sylt
- White Porch Gallery, Miami, USA

2016
- Kunstverein Coburg
- CONTEXT New York, USA
- Stadtlandkunst. Forum für Kulturwelten, Hamburg

2015
- CONTEXT ART MIAMI, USA
- Galerie Hafenliebe, Hamburg

2014
- Kunstverein Schwetzingen, WELDE Publikumspreis / WELDE Audience Award
- Art Market Budapest, Ungarn / Hungary

2013
- Contemporary Istanbul, Türkei / Turkey
- White Porch Gallery, Provincetown, USA
- Wasserturm Mannheim, Wahrzeichen der Stadt Mannheim / Landmark of the city of Mannheim

2012
- art KARLSRUHE
- Galerie Tammen, Berlin

2011
- Klinikum Ludwigshafen
- ART.FAIR 21 Köln / Cologne

2010
- Kunstverein Schwetzingen
- Kunstverein Worms

GRUPPENAUSSTELLUNGEN (AUSWAHL)
GROUP EXHIBITIONS (SELECTION)
2010–2024

2024
- POSITIONS Berlin Art Fair
- Sylt Art Fair
- art KARLSRUHE

2023
- Badischer Kunstverein, Karlsruhe
- GALERIE SUPPER, Baden-Baden

2022
- Kunst Zürich, Schweiz / Switzerland
- Kunstverein Schwetzingen

2021
- Art Miami, USA
- Luxembourg Art Week
- Kunstverein Leimen

2020
- POSITIONS Berlin Art Fair
- Badischer Kunstverein, Karlsruhe

2019
- Cheongju Crafts Biennale, Südkorea / South Korea
- Galerie Tammen, Berlin
- MAC Fort Lauderdale, Florida, USA

2018
- Kunstverein Villa Streccius, Landau
- Positions International Art Fair Luxembourg
- White Porch Gallery, Miami

2017
- Kulturzentrum Englische Kirche, Bad Homburg
- art KARLSRUHE
- POSITIONS Berlin Art Fair

2016
- BRAFA Art Fair, Brüssel, Belgien / Brussels, Belgium
- Miami Art Week, USA

2015
- Kunstverein Leimen
- Mac Fine Art, Fort Lauderdale, USA
- Christian Marx Galerie, Düsseldorf

2014
- CONTEXT Art Miami, USA
- Art FAIR Köln / Cologne
- Kunstverein Schwetzingen

2013
- Galerie Biesenbach, Köln / Cologne
- art KARLSRUHE

2012
- Kunstverein Worms
- Galerie Tammen, Berlin

2011
- Badischer Kunstverein, Karlsruhe
- Commerzbank Hamburg

2010
- Kunstverein Schwetzingen

INSTITUTIONEN, MUSEEN, KUNSTVEREINE SEIT 1995 (AUSWAHL)
INSTITUTIONS, MUSEUMS, ART ASSOCIATIONS SINCE 1995 (SELECTION)

- Biblioteca Nazionale Marciana, Venedig / Venice
- Badischer Kunstverein, Karlsruhe
- Europäisches Parlament, Brüssel, Belgien / European Parliament, Brussels, Belgium
- Coral Springs Museum of Art, Florida, USA
- Museum Pfalzgalerie, Kaiserslautern
- Galerie der Volksbank Kurpfalz eG, Weinheim
- Hauptfeuerwache Mannheim
- Wilhelm-Hack-Museum, Ludwigshafen
- Museum Baden, Solingen-Gräfrath
- Kunstverein Worms
- Salon d'Automne International de Lunéville, Frankreich / France
- Fruchthallen, Kaiserslautern
- Hochschule Pforzheim
- Kulturstiftung Rhein-Neckar-Kreis e. V., Dilsberg
- Kunstverein Leimen
- Kunstverein Schwetzingen
- Galerie der Hoechst AG, Frankfurt am Main
- Kunstverein Villa Streccius in Landau e. V.
- Landesgartenschau Hockenheim
- Mannheimer Kunstverein
- Commerzbank, Hamburg
- Museum Blau, Schwetzingen
- Commerzbank, Mannheim
- Museum für Technik + Arbeit, Mannheim
- MS Europa 2
- Nationaltheater Mannheim
- Volksbank, Weil der Stadt
- Reiß-Museum, Mannheim

DANK
ACKNOWLEDGMENTS

Ich bedanke mich für die hervorragende Zusammenarbeit und die wertvolle Unterstützung bei allen nachfolgenden Personen:
I would like to thank the following people for their excellent cooperation and valuable support:

Dr. Stefano Trovato
Dirk Geuer
Dr. Tayfun Belgin
Dr. Stefano Campagnolo
Margherita Venturelli
Silvia Pugliese
Sebastian Steinhäußer
Janine Campbell-John
Nico Overkott
Serhat Emrullai
Kerstin Ludolph
Katja Durchholz
Judith Kárpáty
Edgar Endl
Federica Rotondo
Tania Morrocchi
Annette Zierer
Daniel Brixy
Nina Fernandez-Westenfelder
David Richardson
Luca Ohlerich

Dietmar Brixy

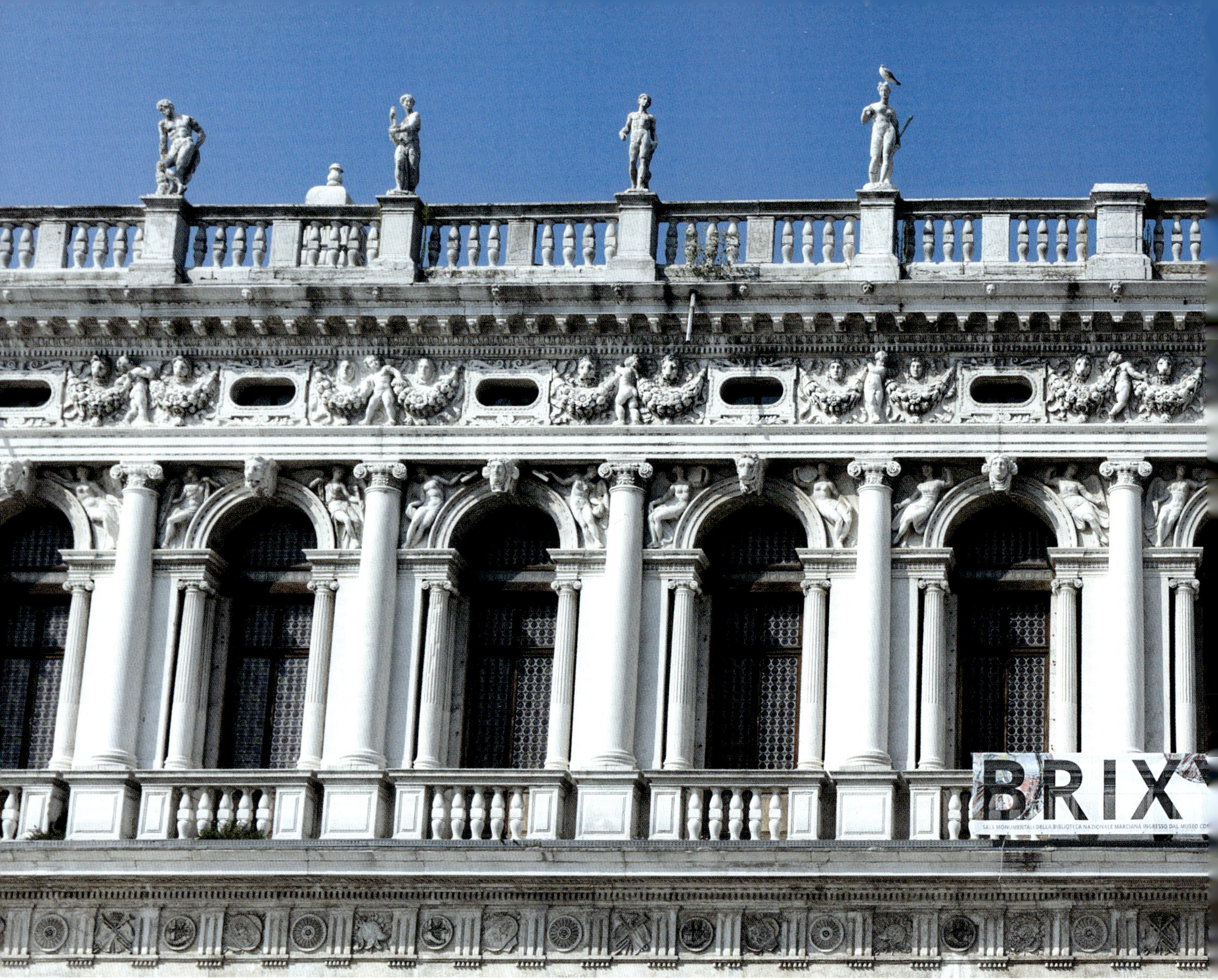

IMPRESSUM / COLOPHON

Ausstellung / Exhibition
The Description of the World
Dietmar Brixy
Biblioteca Nazionale Marciana
Piazza San Marco, 7
I-30124 Venezia
www.bibliotecanazionalemarciana.cultura.gov.it

Direktor / Director: Dr. Stefano Trovato
Kuratoren / Curators: Dr. Tayfun Belgin, Dirk Geuer

Ausstellungsorganisation / Exhibition organisation: Sebastian Steinhäußer, Daniel Brixy, Nina Fernandez-Westenfelder
Koordination / Coordination: Daniel Brixy, Nina Fernandez-Westenfelder, David Richardson, Janine Campbell-John, Margherita Venturelli, Monica Fontana, Federica Rotondo, Sebastian Steinhäußer
Information about artworks / Artwork Info:
Öl auf Nessel / oil on nettle, Acryl auf Papier / acrylic on paper

Katalog / Catalog
Redaktion / Text editor: Sebastian Steinhäußer
Projektmanagement / Project management, Hirmer:
Katja Durchholz, Judith Kárpáty
Gestaltung und Produktion / Graphic design & production:
Daniel Brixy, Edgar Endl (booklab), Nina Fernandez-Westenfelder
Deutsches Korrektorat / German Proof-reading: Susanne Ibisch
Englisches Korrektorat / English Proof-reading: Olivia Parkes
Übersetzung / Translation: Lance Anderson, Elisabetta De Iaco, Madeleine LaRue

Bildrechte / Photo credits: © Alle Kunstwerke und Bilder von / all artworks and images by Dietmar Brixy & Nina Fernandez-Westenfelder, wenn nicht anders angegeben / unless otherwise specified. S. / pp.: Christian Borth, 105; Christian Dammert, 88; Dorothee Piroelle, 23; Maike Müller, 37, 50/51; Peter Schlör, 26; © su concessione della Biblioteca Nazionale Marciana, Venezia: Tiziano, La Sapienza, 38 e immagini 7, 9, 14, 18/19, 29, 37, 50/51, 70/71, 86/87, 112

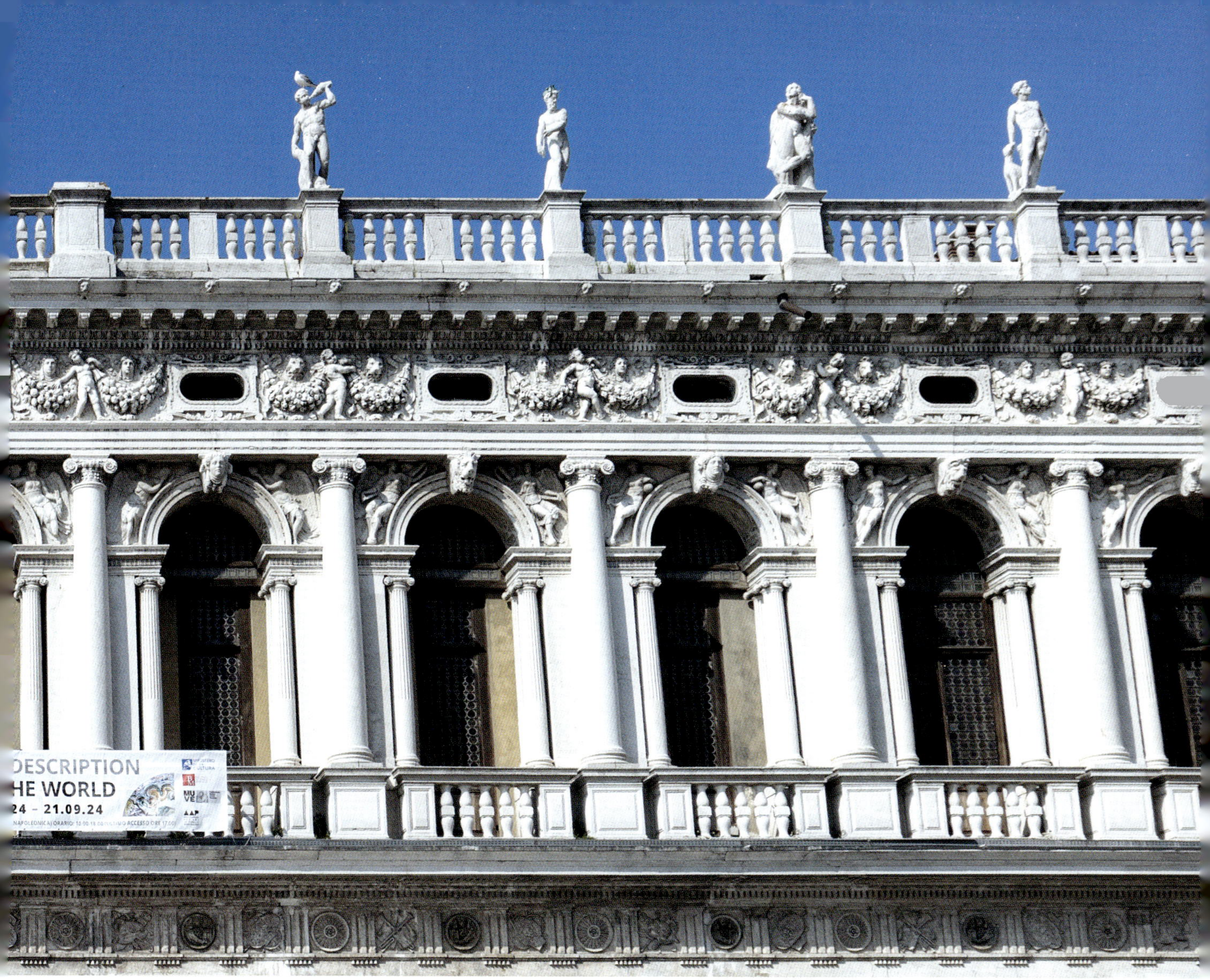

Papier / Paper
Cover: 350g/m² Symbol Card 2side
Innenteil / Inside: 170 g/m² G-Snow
Produktion / Production: Hirmer Verlag GmbH
Druck und Bindung / Printing and binding:
Printer Trento S.r.l, Trento | Printed in Italy

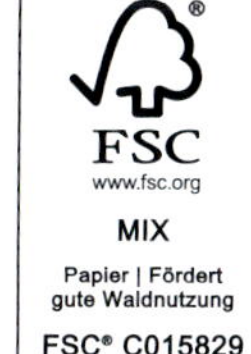

Herausgeber / Publisher
© Association for Art in Public gGmbH
Heinrich-Heine-Allee 19, 40213 Düsseldorf

ISBN 978-3-7774-4479-6

HIRMER VERLAG / HIRMER PUBLISHERS
Geschäftsführerin / Managing Director: Kerstin Ludolph
Bayerstraße 57–59
D-80335 München / Munich
www.hirmerverlag.de / www.hirmerpublishers.com

Bibliografische Information der Deutschen Nationalbibliothek
Die Deutsche Nationalbibliothek verzeichnet diese Publikation in der Deutschen Nationalbibliografie; detaillierte bibliografische Daten sind im Internet über http://www.dnb.de abrufbar.
Bibliographic information published by the Deutsche Nationalbibliothek
The Deutsche Nationalbibliothek lists this publication in the Deutsche Nationalbibliografie; detailed bibliographic data are available in the Internet at http://www.dnb.de.

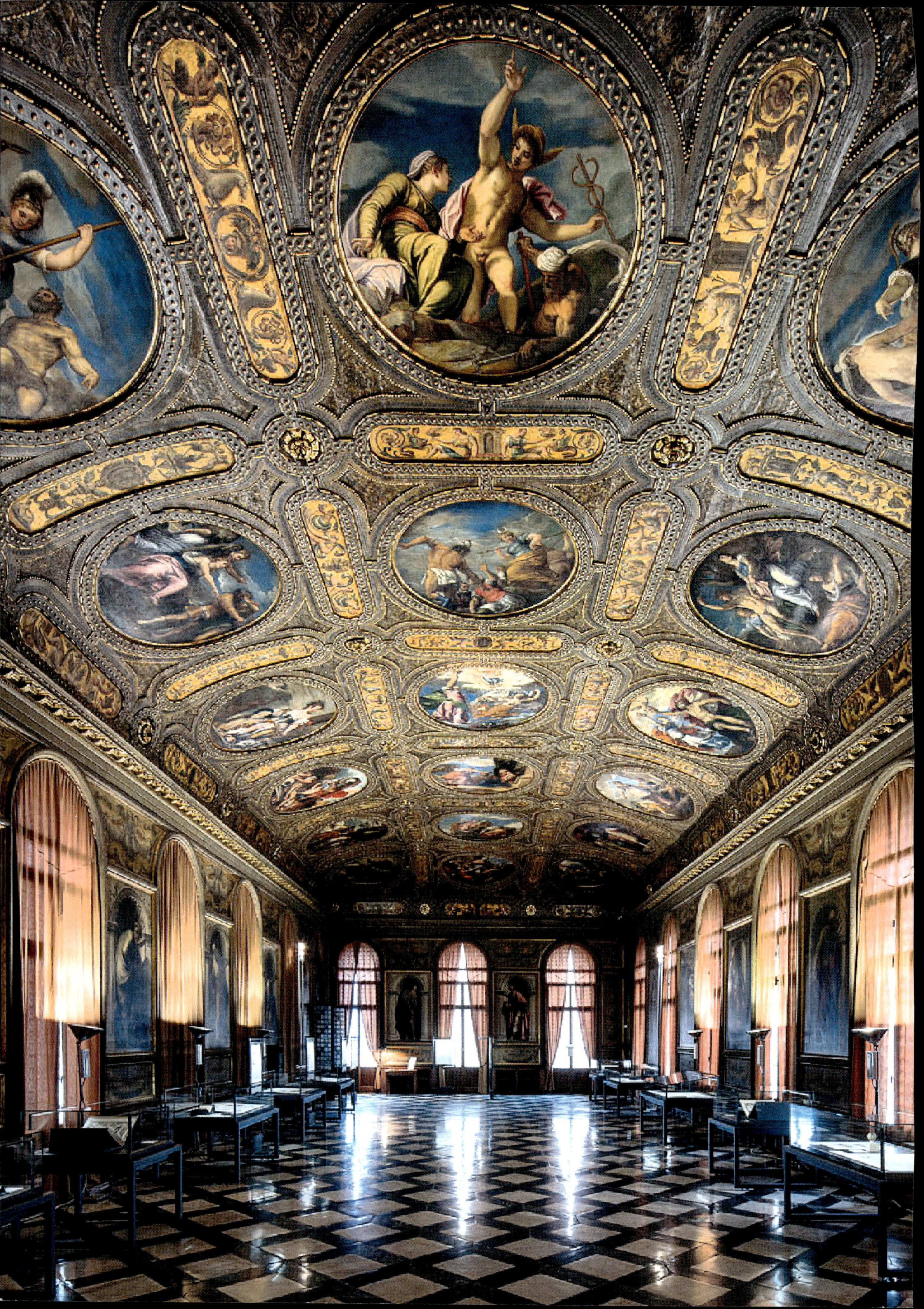